MANAGEMENT LEVEL
PSYCHOMETRIC
& ASSESSMENT
TESTS

More related titles

Handling Tough Job Interviews
Be prepared, perform well, get the job

'Aims to prepare you for anything in job interviews, whether by a recruitment agency, headhunter, employer or human resources department.' – MS London Weekly

Passing Psychometric Tests
Know what to expect and get the job you want

'A very good aid for those who might find themselves facing a psychometric questionnaire.'
– Irish Examiner

Practice Psychometric Tests
Familiarise yourself with genuine recruitment tests and get the job you want

This book will give you the three things you need to pass psychometric tests: information, confidence, and lots and lots of practice.

Successful Interviews Every Time

'The value of Yeung's book ... is that it is clearly written and to the point. To be interviewed without having read it is an opportunity missed.' – The Sunday Times

howtobooks

Please send for a free copy of the latest catalogue:

How To Books
3 Newtec Place, Magdalen Road
Oxford OX4 1RE, United Kingdom
email: info@howtobooks.co.uk
http://www.howtobooks.co.uk

MANAGEMENT LEVEL
PSYCHOMETRIC
& ASSESSMENT
TESTS

Everything

you need to

help you land

that senior job

Andrea Shavick

howto**books**

Published in 2005 by How To Books Ltd,
3 Newtec Place, Magdalen Road,
Oxford OX4 1RE. United Kingdom.
Tel: (01865) 793806. Fax: (01865) 248780.
email: info@howtobooks.co.uk
http://www.howtobooks.co.uk

Andrea Shavick has asserted the right to be identified as the author of this work, in
accordance with the Copyright, Designs and Patents Act 1988.

British Library Cataloguing in Publication Data
A catalogue record for this book is available from the British Library

Cover design by Baseline Arts Ltd, Oxford
Produced for How To Books by Deer Park Productions, Tavistock
Typeset by PDQ Typesetting, Newcastle-under-Lyme, Staffs.
Printed and bound Bell & Bain Ltd, Glasgow

Every effort has been made to trace the copyright holders of material used in this book
but if any have inadvertently been overlooked the publishers will be pleased to make
the necessary arrangements at the first opportunity.

NOTE: The material contained in this book is set out in good faith for general
guidance and no liability can be accepted for loss or expense incurred as a result of
relying in particular circumstances on statements made in the book. The laws and
regulations are complex and liable to change, and readers should check the current
position with the relevant authorities before making personal arrangements.

Contents

Acknowledgements

My thanks to the following people for their help and advice: Ben Maynard, James Bywater, Jane Rutt and Shauna McVeigh of SHL Group plc, Graham Shavick, and Nikki Read of How To Books Ltd.

Introduction – What is Included in This Book

OK so you've applied for that dream job; sent off the CV, filled in the application forms, made the initial phone calls...but wait a minute. What's all this about *psychometric tests*, *personality questionnaires*, *management tests, management exercises* and two day *assessment centre* appointments? Do you really have to jump through all these hoops before they'll even interview you, let alone offer you a management job?

The good news is there are thousands of brilliant firms out there, offering everything from sky-high salaries, profit-related bonuses, long holidays, flexible working, staff discounts, free shares, free canteens, health and life insurance, advanced training, gyms, outings, holidays, not to mention the job satisfaction and level of responsibility you've always know you could handle. But the reality is that the days when all you needed to land a top job was a great CV and a sparkling performance at an interview are long gone. Now you must also pass a whole range of psychometric and management tests with flying colours. And that's what this book is all about.

In Part One of this book I explain all there is to know about **psychometric tests**: what they are, what they measure, why they're used, where and when you'll be taking them, how many you'll take, and how to fill them in correctly. I also include plenty of the most popular management-level practice psychometric tests (verbal, numerical and abstract reasoning) for you to try out in the comfort of your own home, with lots of tips on how to improve your overall performance within each category of test.

Part Two covers just about everything you'll need to know about **Assessment Events** and **Assessment Centres,** including what the difference is between the two. This section includes tips on preparing for your assessment appointment, what to take, what to wear, how to get there on time and how to behave when you do.

One of the best ways to prepare for your assessment centre visit is to **research your target organisation** beforehand, and I devote an entire chapter helping you to do just that. Researching also is a very useful skill to have when you need to prepare a presentation.

Following on from this, I then come to the **management tests and exercises** (or 'business simulations' as they are sometimes called). These are discussed in detail, with tips and helpful advice on how to improve your performance. This section includes plenty of practice with popular management tests such as *Brainstorm, Fastrack,* and *Scenarios,* presentations, in-tray exercises, role-plays, group discussions, interviews and much more.

In **Part Three** I go on to explain everything you need to know about **personality questionnaires**, including the tricky subjects of honesty and whether or not it's possible to cheat. You will also get a chance to familiarise yourself with the universally accepted *OPQ 32* questionnaire.

Finally, if all this testing sounds too much like hard work, then **Part Four** covers the subject of **how to avoid the assessment process** altogether.

By the way, the 35 tests (and over 300 questions) in this book are not 'made up' tests that you sometimes see in books about psychometrics or management, nor are they puzzles or quizzes of the magazine variety. They are genuine practice psychometric and management tests from the biggest test publisher in the world, SHL Group plc. This is the real thing. This is what you'll be facing when you apply for a job with almost any medium-large size company, irrespective of industry, whether private or public sector, and especially if your applying for a senior job.

My aim in writing this book is to give you both knowledge and experience, not just to survive, but to pass real live psychometric and management tests with flying colours. Landing a management job used to be stressful – but not any more!

Andrea Shavick
2005

www.shavick.com

PART ONE
Psychometric Tests

CHAPTER ONE

What are Psychometric Tests?

What are psychometric tests?

Psychometric tests are structured tests, taken in exam-like conditions, which aim to measure objectively a person's ability or certain aspects of their personality. With the exception of personality questionnaires, psychometric tests are always strictly timed.

Psychometric tests are used by thousands of companies worldwide to select and recruit staff at all levels – from shop-floor to managing director. If you're after a job in management, chances are you'll be taking one or more psychometric test.

What do psychometric tests measure?

There are many, many different types of psychometric test. Some measure your ability to understand the written word, or to reason with numbers. Others measure your ability to solve mechanical problems, or follow instructions accurately, or be able to understand data presented in a variety of ways. And then there are the personality questionnaires, assessing everything from motivation to leadership qualities to working preferences. More on this in **Chapter Eleven.**

But psychometric tests cannot measure everything. For example, they can't properly measure conscientiousness, dedication, enthusiasm or loyalty. Personally, I think these qualities are to a large extent, determined by how much you enjoy the actual work, how well you get on with your colleagues, and how decent your boss is. Perhaps they should invent a psychometric test for employers!

Who uses psychometric tests?

At the time of writing, well over 95% of the FTSE 100 companies use psychometric testing to select their staff, as do the police, the Civil Service, local authorities, the Armed Forces, the Fire Service and even the National Health Service, financial institutions, retail sector companies, the motor industry, the IT industry, management consultants, airlines, the power industry...the list is endless.

In fact, virtually every large or medium sized organisation in the UK uses psychometric testing as part of their recruitment process, irrespective of industry. Furthermore, the use of psychometric tests is widespread in Europe, Australia and the USA. The truth is the days of landing a senior management job with just an impressive CV and a good performance at interview are well and truly over.

Why are psychometric tests used?

It makes sense for an employer to find out whether an applicant is capable of doing a job *before* he or she is offered that job. As you probably already know, the whole process of recruiting staff is extremely expensive and time consuming. In fact, for most employers, it's a total nightmare, primarily because it's too easy to pick the wrong person.

Offering a job which involves figure work to a person who turns out to be unable to use a calculator, would be a disaster, as would employing a person in a customer service role who turns out to be bad-tempered and rude. But recruiting the wrong person into a *senior* management position could do incalculable damage, the effects of which may not be realised until it's too late.

The truth is that employers have been employing the wrong people for centuries. The difference is, in the 21st century we have tough employment laws which make it nearly impossible for companies to sack people whenever they feel like it. Employee rights, plus the very real risk of being taken to an industrial tribunal make it even more imperative for employers to choose the right people, first time round – especially when it comes to the most senior positions.

The arrival of the psychometric test (not to mention the multitude of management exercises and 'behavioural simulations') has been embraced by many employers because it gives them an additional tool, over and above the traditional methods of interviewing, studying CVs and taking references. Psychometric tests give employers more confidence in their ability to pick the right people.

Another reason why psychometric tests are used so extensively, especially by large organisations, is because they can be a quick, easy and relatively cheap way of eliminating large numbers of unsuitable candidates early in the recruitment process. At the click of a mouse, candidates at all levels, from shop-floor to managing director, can be tested, short-listed or eliminated more or less instantly.

By 'screening out' unsuitable candidates in one fell swoop, the organisation can then concentrate on the remaining candidates in the hope of finding the 'right' people as quickly as possible.

Yet *another* reason why psychometric tests are so popular is because HR people like using them. From their point of view, psychometric tests have many advantages. First of all the use of psychometric testing can reduce their work load considerably. Why interview 1000 people, when within an hour, you can whittle this number down to the 20 highest calibre candidates?

You also have to remember that HR staff are human beings, with all the same neuroses and self-doubt the rest of us have. When your job is to recruit staff (and your neck will be on the line if you make a hash of it) it's nice to have a scientific and supposedly fail-safe method at your disposal. What better way to reassure yourself that you've got it right?

If nothing else, psychometric tests give HR people (and anyone else who is involved in recruiting staff) something to talk about in an interview. This especially applies to personality tests. For example, if the results of your test indicate you have leadership potential, your interviewer might ask whether you agree with this and ask you to describe situations in which you have used leadership skills. Not only is it useful information for them, it also makes for a more interesting and productive discussion.

When will I have to take a psychometric test?

At any stage in the recruitment process, including first contact. These days many employers are so enthusiastic about psychometric tests, they put them on their application forms and websites (see **Chapter Two – Online Testing**). Psychometric tests are also likely to pop up later in the process when you go along to an 'assessment event' or 'assessment centre' or even an old-fashioned interview appointment.

Note: '*assessment centre*' is HR (Human Resources/Personnel) jargon for getting a small group of the most promising candidates together, either at the employer's premises or an outside location such as a hotel, and subjecting them to an intensive battery of tests, exercises and 'behavioural simulations'. These could include role playing, in-tray exercises, group exercises and discussions, presentations, and of course lots of psychometric tests.

I discuss the delights of the assessment event and the assessment centre (which are different things!) and all the various management tests and exercises in **Part Two** of this book.

What type of psychometric tests will I have to take?

For management jobs, you're most likely to come up against four main types of test, which are:

◆ verbal reasoning
◆ numerical reasoning
◆ abstract reasoning
◆ personality questionnaires.

Verbal, numerical and personality tests are the most popular with employers in the market to recruit managers, however abstract reasoning tests are also used extensively because they're often considered to be a very good indicator of a person's general intellectual ability.

Note: If you want to practise more vocational-related tests such as spatial reasoning, mechanical comprehension, fault diagnosis or accuracy tests, you'll need one of my three other books; *Passing Psychometric Tests*, *Psychometric Tests for Graduates* or *Practice Psychometric Tests* all published by How To Books Ltd.

What's the pass mark?

All organisations using psychometric tests decide their own pass marks (which means there isn't a definitive answer to this question). For lower-level jobs, many organisations set the 'pass' level as low as 50%, especially where the requirement is to use the testing to eliminate candidates who are totally hopeless.

However when you get up to management level, things are a little different. If you are applying for, say, a senior position in finance, it wouldn't be acceptable for your numerical reasoning scores to come in on the low side. For senior jobs you *do* need a high score.

This isn't the same thing as being able to finish the test. In fact many management-level tests are so difficult that nobody ever completes all the questions. But what you do complete needs to be pretty accurate (and there's nothing like lots of practice when it comes to improving your scores).

Of course, each individual test forms a small part of the overall picture; if you get a low score in one test, you could redeem yourself with a good performance in the management tests.

Where will I have to go to take a psychometric test?

For both ability-type tests and personality questionnaires you could be examined at your potential new employer's office, at an assessment centre, at an employment agency office, or in the comfort of your own home using your computer.

Tests taken via the Internet are called 'online tests' and these are discussed in the next chapter.

Note: Information on test and answer format is given in **Chapter Three – In the Exam Room.**

Are psychometric tests fair?

Most psychometric tests which measure ability, and virtually all accredited psychometric tests which measure the many different aspects of personality, are devised by occupational psychologists. Their aim is twofold: to provide employers with a reliable method of selecting the best applicant, and to design tests carefully so that they are as fair as possible.

All psychometric tests, except personality tests, have clear right and wrong answers and are therefore free from the interpretation bias found in the marking of essay-type exam questions. And all applicants for the same job take the same tests. So yes, I would say they are fair. However, if English is not your first language or you're dyslexic, it may be a good idea to declare this before taking the test. The organisation might allow you extra time or grade your results more appropriately.

Test materials can also be adapted for the visually or hearing impaired, but only if you alert the assessors of your circumstances in advance.

Do other industries use psychometric tests?

Psychometric tests have been used for decades in two main fields other than recruitment. These are career guidance, and education.

In career guidance, psychometric tests are used to help individuals gain a better understanding of their own abilities, aptitudes, interests and motivations – obviously very useful information when choosing or changing career. Here, psychometric tests are not used as a selection tool.

However, in education, it's a different ball game. Here, psychometric tests are used by many educational establishments to select the most able pupils. Every year, hundreds of thousands of children as young as 10 sit verbal, numerical and abstract reasoning tests in order to gain entrance to the school of their (or their parents') choice. Whole armies of after-hours teachers have for years been making a living tutoring them.

It seems that whether you're job-hunting or school-hunting, when it comes to psychometric tests, familiarisation and practice is the name of the game.

Once I've got the job, will I have to take any more tests?

Quite possibly. Organisations which use tests to recruit, often use them later on for internal team selection and career development of individual staff members.

How can I improve my psychometric test scores?

Practice, practice, practice. That's what this book is all about. It's amazing how far you can improve your test scores with a bit of practice, especially if you haven't taken many psychometric tests before. Practice also:

◆ Familiarises you with the slightly weird and wonderful psychometric test format so that you know exactly how to correctly record your answers on the day.

◆ Takes away the fear factor, because you'll know what sort of questions to expect.

◆ Gets you used to working under time pressure.

◆ Trains your brain to concentrate – something most of us find very difficult to do for long periods of time.

◆ Speeds you up.

◆ Enables you to pinpoint your strengths, which will give you confidence – and your weaknesses, which you can then work on.

◆ So read on...

CHAPTER TWO

Online Testing

What is an online test?

An online test is simply a psychometric test you take sitting at a computer console via the Internet, usually via your chosen employer's website. The questions appear on the screen, and you click your answer choices with the mouse. Personality questionnaires, competency questionnaires, motivation questionnaires and all of the ability-type tests can all be taken online, including those aimed at the very highest levels of management.

Within a few seconds of you finishing the test, your score (for an ability test) or the analysis of your personality is emailed to the examiner.

What type of tests can be taken online?

Personality questionnaires, competency questionnaires, and virtually all ability-type psychometric tests are taken at all levels of difficulty. The only tests which are more or less impossible to administer via the internet are management tests and exercises. You won't encounter these until you are invited to attend an assessment centre (see **Part Two** for this).

How long are online tests?

Most online tests are fairly short, and certainly far shorter than the tests you'll be expected to take if you go along to an assessment event or assessment centre appointment. Having said that, I've seen some online personality questionnaires with over a hundred pages. Be prepared for an aching wrist.

When will I have to take an online test?

Most online tests usually take place right at the very beginning of the recruitment process. Online tests are used to sift applicants at the earliest stage and pinpoint those individuals who may be suitable.

Where will I have to go to take an online test?

Only as far as the nearest computer connected to the internet. Candidates take online tests at home, in career offices, in employment agencies, on tropical beaches...

What are the advantages of online testing?

For you, it means no worries about getting anywhere on time, and no worries about what to wear. Since you can take an online test any time of the day or night, you won't need to take time off work, or even get dressed! Plus, you should find out if the organisation is interested in taking your application any further within a few minutes, which is a million times better than waiting for them to snail-mail you a letter.

The obvious advantage for the employer is that the candidate doesn't have come into the office. They can take the test at work, at university, in a career office, at a recruitment agency, or even in the comfort of their own home. Instead of spending money 'entertaining' large numbers of candidates, the employer can whittle down the numbers without having to lift a finger. And when you consider that for some graduate recruitment programmes and lower-level management positions the most popular employers receive literally thousands of applications, the cheapness and convenience of online testing is irrefutable. It's certainly becoming more and more popular.

Another advantage for international firms is that they can test candidates anywhere in the world.

How does online testing work?

♦ Simply surf to the website of the company to which you are interested in applying.

♦ Look for a link through to 'recruitment' or if that isn't available, click on 'company information' which normally includes the relevant part of the site.

♦ Skip through the blurb about how wonderful it is to work there (although see **Chapter Eight** on researching companies) and click on the area of work you're interested in.

♦ Follow the instructions on screen, typing your details in the relevant boxes. If the application form asks for a lot of very detailed information, print out a copy and consider your answers carefully before filling in the real thing online.

♦ Once you've registered your details and/or filled in the application form, you will usually receive an acknowledgement and some sort of password which is used to activate the test, and then the assessment process will begin.

♦ When you get to the test, read the questions carefully and click your answer choices with the mouse. **Work quickly because most tests are set to time out after a certain period of time.** This is to prevent you consulting your dictionary, your physics manual, or your best mate – more on this below.

♦ Make sure you answer all the questions. If there are any you really can't do, take an educated guess. Never leave a question unanswered.

♦ Within a few seconds of you finishing the test, your score (for an ability test) or the analysis of your personality is emailed to the examiner. Tests are usually marked automatically, so it's very fast. Many employers will let you know the result within a few days, or even immediately.

Note: Even if you apply for a job in writing or on the telephone, you may still be directed to an online test before you can progress further with your application. Some companies prefer to set a date and time for an online test once you've made contact. You will then sit down at the computer at the designated time, log on to their website using a pre-arranged password, and take your test. Practice psychometric tests begin in **Chapter Four**.

Can online tests be downloaded and then worked on at my own pace?

No. Most psychometric tests have time limits, and the ones you take online are no exception. You must work quickly because they are usually designed to time out after the allotted period of time. This is to prevent you looking up the answers at your leisure, consulting your physics manual, or your best mate. And speaking of cheating...

Cheating – is it possible?

Tempting, isn't it? If your prospective employer can't actually see you, how do they know it's *you* taking the test and not your genius of a best mate? Or that she isn't sitting next to you, helpfully prompting you with the answers?

The answer is, they can't. However, if cheating does succeed in getting you further along the recruitment road, the chances are that you'll be found out. Practically all companies who use online testing *retest* successful candidates further down the line, either at an assessment event or at interview. So if your online test score is dazzling but your interview test score is depressing, they'll know why.

So be warned – your online test will *not* be the only psychometric test you will be taking. HR people are not stupid. Knowing how easy it is to cheat in the online test, many companies deliberately pick a selection of candidates, and with them safely inside the assessment centre or company premises, they spring the same test on them! If you cheated the first time, you'll get rumbled.

More on the perils of test cheating are explained in **Chapter Eleven** on **Personality Tests** and in **Chapter Seven – Assessment Events and Assessment Centres**.

CHAPTER THREE

In the Exam Room

This chapter explains how to make the most of your time in the actual examination room as well as how to fill in a psychometric test paper. The practice psychometric tests themselves are coming up in the next three chapters.

One thing that does need to be said is that just because you are a manager, (or nearly one) doesn't mean that you'll sail through every test that is thrown at you without any problems. Some you'll find easy, but some will definitely give you a hard time.

Hopefully the following tips and exam techniques will help you make the most of your time in the exam room, especially if you haven't ventured inside one since you left school.

Listen carefully

When you are taking psychometric tests, or any sort of test for that matter, you *must* listen very carefully to the test administrator's instructions. Pay particular attention to what they say about the end of the test. *Unlike academic exams,* the administrator may not be allowed to warn candidates that time's nearly up.

Ask questions first

If there is anything about the test instructions you do not understand, or you have any other problem at all, then the time to ask is before it starts. Once the clock is ticking no interruptions will be allowed. Although I guess it's acceptable to tell the administrator that half your test paper is missing. It does happen.

Check out the paper

Instead of plunging straight into the test, have a quick check through the paper so you can see what you're up against. Is there a separate answer sheet? How many questions are there? How many different sections? What about the time limits?

Plenty of people have sat smugly in exam rooms congratulating themselves on how speedily they finished the paper, only to discover that they've missed the last page. That really is a horrible feeling, but by checking out the paper *first* you won't have a problem.

Pace yourself

Pacing yourself is all about working through the paper at the right speed. Too fast and your accuracy will suffer. Too slow and you'll run out of time.

Once you've looked at the test paper, try to estimate how much time you have to answer each question, for example 50 questions in 25 minutes equals 30 seconds each. Once you've done this you'll know that after 10 minutes you should have tackled around 20 questions, and after 20 minutes you should have tackled around 40 questions and so on. As you work through the paper, check your progress from time to time. This should ensure you never get too far behind, and also reassure you that you're doing OK.

Note: Sometimes ability-type tests such as numerical reasoning become harder as you go along, so consider leaving more time for the later questions.

One tricky situation that can occur is when you come up against a question that you simply cannot answer, either because it's too difficult or the wording seems ambiguous. If you only have around 30 seconds per question, you can see that spending 10 minutes figuring out a tough one out is a bad idea. So if you get stuck, don't give yourself a hard time, simply give it up and move on. If you make a tiny mark next to the unanswered question (or ring the question number) you'll be able to see at a glance which questions still need tackling. If you have any time at the end, you can go back and try again.

As for any ambiguity, be assured recruiters are not out to trick you. Professionally authored psychometric tests do not include any trick questions. Having said that, it does sometimes happen that a question is poorly worded, or the answer choices have been misprinted. Just let it go, take an educated guess and move on.

Read the questions

Read each question or set of instructions very carefully so that you know exactly what information you're being asked for. This might sound totally obvious, but when you're under stress it's very tempting to rush and not bother to check what you're being asked to do. Many people (myself included) are so used to scanning through chunks of text at high speed, they find reading every single word incredibly difficult. So slow down and concentrate.

Record your answers accurately

Psychometric tests usually come in a multiple choice format. This means you will be given four or five possible answers choices for each question. Once you have decided which is the correct one, mark the corresponding box or circle on the answer sheet accordingly. An example of how to do this will usually given at the beginning of the paper.

It is vitally important that you follow these directions precisely. If you are asked to fill in the box or circle, **fill it in completely**. Don't just make a little squiggle inside it, or tick it or put a cross through it.

The reason this is so important is because most psychometric tests are marked either by computers using a technique called optical marking, or an 'answer grid' which the test administrator positions over the answer sheet.

Either way, if you record your answers in the correct way, the computer (or test administrator) will be able to 'read' them. If you don't, you'll lose points – even if your answers are correct.

The same goes for the number of answers required. If you are asked to mark one circle, mark only one circle. If you mark two, the computer or test administrator will not know which is your intended correct answer, and you'll lose a mark, even if one of the answers is correct.

If you take the tests on a computer or laptop, you'll find that generally the program will not allow you to click more than the required number of answer choices.

Work through the questions in order

Some people skip through test papers looking for questions they know they'll be able to answer easily. The trouble with this is that it wastes time, it's better to work through the paper in order. As I explained above, if you can't answer a question, mark it and move on to the next one. At the end, if you have time, you can have another go.

Use tried and tested exam techniques

◆ Try to work out the correct answer before looking at any of the answer choices. That way, even if you can't come up with a definite answer, you'll be able to make an educated guess.

◆ Narrow your choices by immediately eliminating answers that you can see are incorrect.

◆ If you think a question could be a 'trick' question, think again. Psychometric tests are always straightforward, there are never questions intended to deceive. It could be that you're reading too much into the question; instead try to take it at face value.

◆ Only change your answer if you are absolutely sure you have answered incorrectly. First answers are usually the correct ones.

◆ Keep working through the paper at a steady pace, keeping an eye on the clock.

Concentrate

Many people find it difficult to concentrate intensely for long periods of time, however senior or professional they are. It isn't easy to block out everything around you and work non-stop for up to an hour without a break. Even if you are working in a quiet room without disturbance, your mind can start to wander all too easily.

The best way to combat this is to take a very short break. Sit up straight, shut your eyes and take two or three long slow breaths. Or try resting your eyes by focusing them on a point in the far distance for about ten seconds.

Don't panic

You're almost out of time and you've got that horrible sinking feeling that says, 'Help! I'm not going to finish!' Don't panic. Instead, reassure yourself with these facts:

1   You don't have to score 100% to pass. Pass rates are determined by the recruiting organisation and depend on a multitude of factors, including the number of candidates and the skills needed to actually carry out the job, but it's rare for any candidate to score full marks. Do your best and don't give yourself a hard time.

2   Many psychometric tests are not designed to be finished in the time set. Giving you more questions than you can reasonably cope with in the allotted time is a deliberate ploy. Taking a psychometric test is meant to be stressful! Afterwards, if any of the other candidates boast about finishing 15 minutes ahead of the rest of the room – they're probably lying.

3   In management recruiting, a candidate's scores in the ability-type psychometric tests form just a part of the overall picture. Your performance in the management tests and exercises are just as important.

How to get the best out of this book

To get the best out this book, treat the practice tests as if you were taking them in a real live interview situation. In other words, sit somewhere quiet, without distractions, and work as quickly and as accurately, and with as much concentration as you can. If you find it tough going don't worry, as the more you try, the easier it will become.

Work through each test in its entirety (even if you think some of them are too easy for you) if for no other reason than to train your brain to concentrate. Remember that these tests are *practice* tests – when you apply for a job, the psychometric tests you'll be taking will generally have a lot more questions. Getting used to concentrating now will stand you in good stead and give you an advantage over the other candidates.

Record your answer choices in pencil by filling in completely the appropriate circles on the answer sheet – there's one for each test (except some of the management tests). This will familiarise you with the technique for recording your answers.

Almost all the practice tests have suggested **time limits**. Set the clock, and attempt as many questions as you can in the time allowed, but don't worry if you can't complete all the questions. In the real world, *psychometric tests always have more questions than most people can handle*. It's a deliberate ploy to put you under pressure, to see how you work when under stress. Besides, working under a time constraint is good experience in itself.

Of course, there's nothing to stop you giving yourself more time, or attempting the questions as many times as you like – even after you've checked out the answers. Sometimes the only way to understand a test is to look at it with the answers in front of you!

Psychometric test list

If you want to practise a particular type of psychometric test, the following list will help you locate the one you want quickly:

At the end of each chapter there is a section dedicated to helping you improve your performance...and the answers of course.

Why these three types of ability test?

Verbal reasoning, numerical reasoning and to a lesser extent, abstract reasoning are the three ability-type psychometric tests you will encounter when you apply for a managerial job.

Other ability-type psychometric tests (such as fault diagnosis, mechanical comprehension, spatial reasoning and accuracy/acuity tests) are generally used in the selection of candidates where those specific skills are required. For example, for IT positions and technical roles you are likely to encounter the full range of spatial reasoning, fault diagnosis and mechanical comprehension tests; for clerical jobs the accuracy tests are extremely useful. If you want to practise these types of test then you'll need one of my three other psychometric books – *Passing Psychometric Tests, Psychometric Tests for Graduates,* or *Practice Psychometric Tests.* All three are published by How To Books Ltd.

Note: Personality and **management tests and management exercises** (all a vital part of the recruitment process into management) are covered in detail later in this book.

Remember – familiarisation and practice is the name of the game! Good luck.

CHAPTER FOUR

Verbal and Critical Reasoning

Verbal reasoning tests are multiple choice tests which measure your ability to reason with words. They are widely used in recruitment to select staff at all levels, simply because the ability to understand the written word is an essential skill for most jobs.

The simplest verbal reasoning tests assess your basic language skills: spelling, vocabulary and understanding of grammar. You are usually presented with four or five different words, or groups of words, and asked to pick the ones which:

✓ Are spelt correctly.
✓ Are spelt incorrectly.
✓ Do not belong in the group.
✓ Mean the same.
✓ Mean the opposite.
✓ Best complete a sentence.
✓ Best fill the gaps in a sentence.

Here's a couple of easy examples:

Choose the words which **best** complete the following sentences:

All employees should.................from such a training scheme.

A. result   B. credit   C. succeed   D. enrol   E. benefit

The insurance.................will.................if you do not pay on time.

A. pollicy   B. pollicy   C. polisy   D. polisy   E. none of these
   laps   lapse   lapps   lapsed

You are being tested on your vocabulary, spelling and grammatical skills, and this type of test can range from basic school leaver to management level. The answers, of course, are both E.

Analogies are also popular. Author is to book, as artist is to:

A. paintbrush
B. gallery
C. painting
D. picture frame.

What's being tested here is your ability to recognise relationships between words. If an author *creates* a book, what might an artist create? The correct answer is C. There are examples of this type of test in two of my previous books on psychometrics; *Passing Psychometric Tests*, and *Practice Psychometric Tests.*

For higher-level jobs, however, the tests become more difficult. Here your ability to make sense of, and logically evaluate the written word, is examined, for obvious reasons. The ability to understand, consider and logically evaluate complex information is an absolutely essential qualification for most managerial positions.

These higher-level tests are often called **critical reasoning** tests but in essence they are comprehension exercises. In each case you are required to read a short text, or passage and then answer questions about it. However, unlike the comprehension exercises that you did in school, where the answers were obvious so long as you read the text carefully enough, critical reasoning tests generally require a little more brain power.

You are often asked to decide whether a statement is true or false, or impossible to verify, *given the information contained in the passage.* This last phrase is very important. Not only are you being forced to think very carefully about what you have read, you must endeavour not make any assumptions about it. You must answer the question using only the given information – something which is surprisingly difficult to do if you have any knowledge of (or an opinion on) the subject matter in question. Remember, it is only your ability to understand and make logical deductions from the passage that is being tested, not your knowledge of the subject matter.

The vocabulary and subject of the passage are often similar to those encountered in the job for which you are applying. For example, if you are applying for a management job in IT, then any critical reasoning test you encounter is quite likely to include the language, vocabulary and jargon prevalent in that industry. But whatever type of vocabulary is used, the level of understanding required is pretty high.

All verbal reasoning/critical reasoning psychometric tests are strictly timed, and *every single question will have one, and only one correct answer.*

In this chapter there are 11 different verbal reasoning and critical reasoning practice tests for you to try, of varying difficulty. All of them are used to select candidates for managerial jobs, from graduate recruits up to senior management levels.

At the very end of the chapter there is section entitled **Verbal and critical reasoning tests – how to improve your performance,** which is intended to help you do just that across the whole range of verbal and critical reasoning tests. Included in this section are some hints on tackling the questions themselves. If you have a problem with any of the questions then hopefully the advice contained in this section will get you back on track. Remember however that all of us have strengths and weaknesses, and everyone will have some difficulty with some of the tests in this book.

Test 1 Verbal Application

This test is designed to gauge your ability to understand the meaning of complex words, logic within sentences, and grammar. It is suitable for candidates for junior, middle and senior management jobs over a wide range of industries.

Instructions: Choose the combination of words which you think will best fit the blank spaces for each question. Your answers should be grammatical and make the most sense. For each answer, mark, by filling in completely, the appropriate circle in the answer section.

Time guideline: see how many questions you can answer in 4 minutes.

---

1 The [_____] of the venture might have been predicted if [_____] attention had been paid to the report which pinpointed several fundamental problems.

A	B	C	D	E
failure	failure	failure	success	success
no	less	more	more	greater

---

2 The problem is not so [_____] the total amount of funding assigned to the department, but rather that this funding has been [_____] too thinly amongst individual managers.

A	B	C	D	E
much	much	much	uniquely	uniquely
given	spread	focused	assigned	distributed

---

3 The company will provide [_____] clothing and equipment where it is required. However, it is up to the [_____] to take reasonable care of their own safety by using the equipment that is provided.

A	B	C	D	E
protection	protective	protective	protective	precautionary
employed	employment	employers	employees	employees

---

4 The decision was [_____] by the workforce as an important move towards providing a [_____] defined career structure.

A	B	C	D	E
applauded	greeted	criticised	dismissed	welcomed
radically	poorly	poorly	well	well

5

Her first step in [_____] the problem was to [_____] the opinions of those who would actually be involved in the day to day running of the scheme.

A	B	C	D	E
creating	generating	solving	enhancing	identifying
define	imitate	seek	discredit	divulge

6

The job losses came despite [_____] pressure to reverse the demand for [_____] cuts.

A	B	C	D	E
growing	decreasing	increasing	weakening	mounting
tax	job	sales	spending	expenditure

7

[_____] are reminded that all expense [_____] should be authorised by their [_____] and sent to Accounts with the relevant VAT receipt.

A	B	C	D	E
Staff	Staff	Staff	Managers	Managers
forms	allowances	claims	claims	bills
clients	supervisors	supervisors	subordinates	subordinates

8

[_____] recent industrial relations [_____], the company hopes that profits will [_____] a dividend to be paid to the shareholders.

A	B	C	D	E
Despite	Because of	In view of	In line with	Due to
conflicts	set backs	acrimonies	improvements	difficulties
allow	prevent	permit	deter	preclude

Test 1 Answer Sheet

	A	B	C	D	E
1	Ⓐ	Ⓑ	Ⓒ	Ⓓ	Ⓔ
2	Ⓐ	Ⓑ	Ⓒ	Ⓓ	Ⓔ
3	Ⓐ	Ⓑ	Ⓒ	Ⓓ	Ⓔ
4	Ⓐ	Ⓑ	Ⓒ	Ⓓ	Ⓔ
5	Ⓐ	Ⓑ	Ⓒ	Ⓓ	Ⓔ
6	Ⓐ	Ⓑ	Ⓒ	Ⓓ	Ⓔ
7	Ⓐ	Ⓑ	Ⓒ	Ⓓ	Ⓔ
8	Ⓐ	Ⓑ	Ⓒ	Ⓓ	Ⓔ

Test 2 Verbal Evaluation

This test measures your ability to understand and evaluate the logic of various kinds of argument.

This type of test is often used to assess reasoning skills at administrative, supervisory and junior management levels. It could be used to select applicants for a wide range of jobs, for example, sales and customer service staff, junior managers and management trainees.

Instructions: In this test you are required to evaluate each statement in the light of the passage and select your answer according to the rules below:

Mark circle A if the statement follows logically from *the information or opinions contained in the passage*.

Mark circle B if the statement is obviously false from *the information or opinions contained in the passage*.

Mark circle C if you cannot say whether the statement is true or false *without further information*.

Indicate your answer each time by filling in completely the appropriate circle on the answer sheet.

Time guideline: See how many questions you can complete in 5 minutes.

> Many organisations find it beneficial to employ students during the summer. Permanent staff often wish to take their own holidays over this period. Furthermore, it is not uncommon for companies to experience peak workloads in the summer and so require extra staff. Summer employment also attracts students who may return as well qualified recruits to an organisation when they have completed their education. Ensuring that the students learn as much as possible about the organisation encourages their interest in working on a permanent basis. Organisations pay students on a fixed rate without the usual entitlement to paid holidays or sick leave.

1   It is possible that permanent staff who are on holiday can have their work carried out by students.

2   Students in summer employment are given the same paid holiday benefit as permanent staff.

3   Students are subject to the organisation's standard disciplinary and grievance procedures.

4   Some companies have more work to do in summer when students are available for vacation work.

Most banks and building societies adopt a 'no smoking' policy in customer areas in their branches. Plaques and stickers are displayed in these areas to draw attention to this policy. The notices are worded in a 'customer friendly' manner, though a few customers may feel their personal freedom of choice is being infringed. If a customer does ignore a notice, staff are tolerant and avoid making a great issue of the situation. In fact, the majority of customers now expect a 'no smoking' policy in premises of this kind. After all, such a policy improves the pleasantness of the customer facilities and also lessens fire risk.

5   'No smoking' policies have mainly been introduced in response to customer demand.

6   All banks and building societies now have a 'no smoking' policy.

7   There is no conflict of interest between a 'no smoking' policy and personal freedom of choice for all.

8   A no-smoking policy is in line with most customers' expectations in banks and building societies.

Test 2 Answer Sheet

	A	B	C
1	Ⓐ	Ⓑ	Ⓒ
2	Ⓐ	Ⓑ	Ⓒ
3	Ⓐ	Ⓑ	Ⓒ
4	Ⓐ	Ⓑ	Ⓒ
5	Ⓐ	Ⓑ	Ⓒ
6	Ⓐ	Ⓑ	Ⓒ
7	Ⓐ	Ⓑ	Ⓒ
8	Ⓐ	Ⓑ	Ⓒ

Test 3 Verbal Test

This test measures your ability to evaluate the logic of written information. This type of test is used for the selection of graduates over a wide range of industries. It can also be used in the selection and development of work-experienced managers, professional staff and middle managers.

Instructions: In this test you are given two passages, each of which is followed by several statements. You are required to evaluate the statements in the light of the information or opinions contained in the passage and select your answer according to the rules given below:

Mark circle A if the statement is patently true, or follows logically *given the information or opinions contained in the passage.*

Mark circle B if the statement is patently untrue, or if the opposite follows logically, *given the information or opinions contained in the passage.*

Mark circle C if you cannot say whether the statement is true or untrue or follows logically *without further information.*

Indicate your answer each time by filling in completely the appropriate circle on the answer sheet.

Time guideline: There is no official time guideline for this practice test, however try to work through the questions as quickly as you can.

> The big economic difference between nuclear and fossil-fuelled power stations is that nuclear reactors are more expensive to build and decommission, but cheaper to run. So disputes over the relative efficiency of the two systems revolve not just around the prices of coal and uranium today and tomorrow, but also around the way in which future income should be compared with current income.

1   The main difference between nuclear and fossil-fuelled power stations is an economic one.

2   The price of coal is not relevant to discussions about the relative efficiency of nuclear reactors.

3   If nuclear reactors were cheaper to build and decommission than fossil-fuelled power stations, they would definitely have the economic advantage.

> At any given moment we are being bombarded by physical and psychological stimuli competing for our attention. Although our eyes are capable of handling more than 5 million bits of data per second, our brains are capable of interpreting only about 500 bits per second. With similar disparities between each of the other senses and the brain, it is easy to see that we must select the visual, auditory, or tactile stimuli that we wish to compute at any specific time.

4   Physical stimuli usually win in the competition for our attention.

5   The capacity of the human brain is sufficient to interpret nearly all the stimuli the senses can register under optimum conditions.

6   Eyes are able to cope with greater input of information than ears.

Test 3 Answer Sheet

	A	B	C
1	Ⓐ	Ⓑ	Ⓒ
2	Ⓐ	Ⓑ	Ⓒ
3	Ⓐ	Ⓑ	Ⓒ
4	Ⓐ	Ⓑ	Ⓒ
5	Ⓐ	Ⓑ	Ⓒ
6	Ⓐ	Ⓑ	Ⓒ

Test 4 Verbal Evaluation

The following test measures your ability to understand and evaluate the logic of written information and is used in the selection of staff working in a very large range of jobs, including supervisory, customer contact, administration and junior management.

Instructions: In this test you are given two passages, each one followed by several statements. You are required to evaluate each statement in the light of the information or opinions contained in the relevant passage and select your answer according to the rules below:

Mark circle A if the statement is patently true, or follows logically *given the information in the passage.*

Mark circle B if the statement is patently untrue, or if the opposite follows logically, *given the information in the passage.*

Mark circle C if you cannot say whether the statement is true or follows logically *without further information.*

Indicate your answer each time by filling in completely the appropriate circle on the answer sheet.

Time guideline: See how many questions you can complete in 5 minutes.

Course for New Entrants

The induction course had a target of sixty hours, to be run for one hour per day for twelve weeks. The lesson time of one hour was considered to be the best length. It was thought that learning proficiency would fall sharply if lessons were longer and took place less frequently. At the end of the twelve weeks it was hoped that the trainees would have obtained the course objective of building confidence to cope with more complicated situations at work.

1   The course lasted 12 weeks.

2   A lesson time of two hours was considered to be the best length.

3   A target of 90 hours was set for the course.

4   These courses are beneficial to the entire population.

MEMORANDUM

To: All Staff
Date: 22 June
SUBJECT: New Filing Clerk

Despite the enormous strides forward in office automation, the amount of paperwork and consequently the amount of filing, grows and grows. Statistics show that, on average, a secretary spends twenty per cent of working time filing and during the course of one year creates at least five thousand new files. It is therefore this company's policy to employ a full-time filing clerk who will reorganise the filing system more efficiently and cut down the number of files needed by each department, thus freeing individual secretaries from this task.

For further enquiries about the above please telephone Ms Espey on Ext. 247

5 This memo should be distributed to all staff.

6 Statistics show that, on average, a secretary spends a third of working time filing.

7 Ms Espey should be contacted for further enquiries.

8 All firms should employ a full-time filing clerk.

Test 4 Answer Sheet

	A	B	C
1	Ⓐ	Ⓑ	Ⓒ
2	Ⓐ	Ⓑ	Ⓒ
3	Ⓐ	Ⓑ	Ⓒ
4	Ⓐ	Ⓑ	Ⓒ
5	Ⓐ	Ⓑ	Ⓒ
6	Ⓐ	Ⓑ	Ⓒ
7	Ⓐ	Ⓑ	Ⓒ
8	Ⓐ	Ⓑ	Ⓒ

Test 5 Verbal Evaluation

The following test measures your ability to understand and evaluate the logic of written information and is used in the selection of staff working in a very large range of jobs, including supervisory, customer contact, administration and junior management.

Instructions: In this test you are given two passages, each one followed by several statements. You are required to evaluate each statement in the light of the information or opinions contained in the relevant passage and select your answer according to the rules below:

Mark circle A if the statement is patently true, or follows logically *given the information in the passage*.

Mark circle B if the statement is patently untrue, or if the opposite follows logically, *given the information in the passage*.

Mark circle C if you cannot say whether the statement is true or follows logically *without further information*.

Indicate your answer each time by filling in completely the appropriate circle on the answer sheet.

Time guideline: See how many questions you can complete in 5 minutes.

USE OF THE TELEPHONE

The telephone is the executive's most used tool. A survey has shown that, in Britain, executives make around thirty-nine business calls a day in the south, and approximately thirty-one per day in the north. However, fifty-three per cent of the executives surveyed also complained of wasting a lot of time on the phone through waiting for calls, returning calls, or simply not getting through. International telephones are working on a computerised system which should help to eliminate some of these problems, but one should not expect this change within the next decade.

1 According to the survey, executives in the north make around 39 business calls a day.

2 The telephone will always be the executive's most used tool.

3 Over half of the executives in the survey said that they waste a lot of time on the telephone.

4 Telephones are often misused.

> ## SAFARI PARK SAFETY
>
> When visiting a safari park visitors are reminded of the importance of keeping their car windows closed. Many accidents have occurred through visitors winding down their car windows to take photographs. Baboons have then gained access to the car interior with disastrous results. In some cases, the visitors actually step out of the car and take a closer look at the wild animals, resulting in serious injury. Signs warning of these and other dangers are sited every five hundred yards around the park. Safari park advisors are at a loss to know what other measures to take to warn the public of the dangers of wild animals.

5   Visitors sometimes get out of their car to look more closely at the animals.

6   Accidents have occurred when visitors wind down their windows to take photographs.

7   'Danger' signs are placed every 50 yards around the park.

8   The general public should be banned from safari parks.

Test 5 Answer Sheet

	A	B	C
1	Ⓐ	Ⓑ	Ⓒ
2	Ⓐ	Ⓑ	Ⓒ
3	Ⓐ	Ⓑ	Ⓒ
4	Ⓐ	Ⓑ	Ⓒ
5	Ⓐ	Ⓑ	Ⓒ
6	Ⓐ	Ⓑ	Ⓒ
7	Ⓐ	Ⓑ	Ⓒ
8	Ⓐ	Ⓑ	Ⓒ

Test 6 Verbal Evaluation

The following test measures your ability to understand and evaluate the logic of written information and is used in the selection of staff working in a very large range of jobs, including supervisory, customer contact, administration and junior management.

Instructions: In this test you are given two passages, each one followed by several statements. You are required to evaluate each statement in the light of the information or opinions contained in the relevant passage and select your answer according to the rules below:

Mark circle A if the statement is patently true, or follows logically *given the information in the passage.*

Mark circle B if the statement is patently untrue, or if the opposite follows logically, *given the information in the passage.*

Mark circle C if you cannot say whether the statement is true or follows logically *without further information.*

Indicate your answer each time by filling in completely the appropriate circle on the answer sheet.

Time guideline: See how many questions you can complete in 5 minutes.

PASSIVE SMOKING

A few years ago complaints about pollution in the office by tobacco smoke would not have been taken seriously. However, recent evidence published in medical journals suggests that even 'secondary inhalation' (breathing in someone else's smoke) can put non-smokers at an increased risk from the harmful properties of tobacco smoke. This makes them more susceptible to chest and respiratory problems than non-smokers living and working in smoke-free environments.

1 In the past, complaints about tobacco smoke pollution would have been treated seriously.

2 'Secondary inhalation' is breathing in another's smoke.

3 Medical journals have proposed that smoking should be banned from offices.

4 Smokers have an increased risk of heart disease.

> ### How to Encourage a Child's Interest in Education
>
> To help stimulate their child's interest in education, wise parents should become involved starting from the child's first day of school. The child's drawings should be praised and subsequent help given with homework. This should create an enjoyable habit of seeking knowledge for knowledge's sake, rather than a chore to be finished before the child may watch television or go out to play. Close communication between teachers and parents is also beneficial to the child as possible problems on both sides can be discussed and resolved to the child's advantage.

5   Wise parents should praise their child's drawings.

6   Teachers and parents should avoid talking to each other.

7   All children watch television.

8   All children should go to play school.

Test 6 Answer Sheet

	A	B	C
1	Ⓐ	Ⓑ	Ⓒ
2	Ⓐ	Ⓑ	Ⓒ
3	Ⓐ	Ⓑ	Ⓒ
4	Ⓐ	Ⓑ	Ⓒ
5	Ⓐ	Ⓑ	Ⓒ
6	Ⓐ	Ⓑ	Ⓒ
7	Ⓐ	Ⓑ	Ⓒ
8	Ⓐ	Ⓑ	Ⓒ

Test 7 Verbal Evaluation

The following test measures your ability to understand and evaluate the logic of written information and is used in the selection of staff working in a very large range of jobs, including supervisory, customer contact, administration and junior management.

Instructions: In this test you are given one passage, followed by several statements. You are required to evaluate each statement in the light of the information or opinions contained in the passage and select your answer according to the rules below:

Mark circle A if the statement is patently true, or follows logically *given the information in the passage.*

Mark circle B if the statement is patently untrue, or if the opposite follows logically, *given the information in the passage.*

Mark circle C if you cannot say whether the statement is true or follows logically *without further information.*

Indicate your answer each time by filling in completely the appropriate circle on the answer sheet.

Time guideline: See how many questions you can complete in 5 minutes.

Women as Seen on Television

Despite the fact that sixty per cent of Britain's married women have their own careers, fiction and television writers still refer to wives in such terms as 'her indoors' or portray them as downtrodden slaves at the kitchen sink, surrounded by hordes of grubby kids. By comparison, television adverts show sparkling clean kitchens with housewives surrounded by 2.3 freshly scrubbed children in a germ-free environment. Neither of these two descriptions portrays the reality of working married women in today's society: it is thought that until women themselves hold the top posts in the television industry, these views will remain unchanged.

1 Sixty per cent of Britain's married women have their own careers.

2 Television writers never refer to wives as 'her indoors'.

3 Women hold all the top posts in the television industry.

4 The National Statistics show that most couples have 2.3 children.

Test 7 Answer Sheet

	A	B	C
1	Ⓐ	Ⓑ	Ⓒ
2	Ⓐ	Ⓑ	Ⓒ
3	Ⓐ	Ⓑ	Ⓒ
4	Ⓐ	Ⓑ	Ⓒ

Test 8 Critical Reasoning

This test is designed to find out how well you are able to evaluate the logic of various kinds of arguments. It is suitable for candidates for junior, middle and senior management jobs over a wide range of industries.

Instructions: The test consists of a passage, which is followed by several statements. Your task is to read the passage and evaluate each statement according to the following rules:

Mark circle A if the statement must be true based on the information in the passage.

Mark circle B if the statement is definitely false given the information in the passage.

Mark circle C if you cannot say whether the statement is true or false without further information.

Base your answers only on the information given in the passage.

Time guideline: There is no official time limit for this test, just work as fast and as accurately as you can.

Indicate your answer each time by filling in completely the appropriate circle in the answer sheet.

Internet Junkyard

A junkyard may contain endless amounts of rusted metal and heaps of useless items that at one time formed part of something. People visit junkyards looking for replacement parts or something that might just work for a project, yet most of what they see remains where it is. There are parts of the internet that are beginning to resemble a junkyard, cluttered with old sites, the majority of which lost their value long ago. The information available is often outdated and stale. There are businesses that allow their sites to deteriorate into junk and they are missing a great opportunity to gain a competitive advantage.

---

1   Most of the Internet is becoming a junkyard.

2   Despite the fact that items from a junkyard can and will be re-cycled, a lot of it will never be used again.

3   Websites will always lose their value if they are not properly maintained.

Test 8 Answer Sheet

	A	B	C
1	Ⓐ	Ⓑ	Ⓒ
2	Ⓐ	Ⓑ	Ⓒ
3	Ⓐ	Ⓑ	Ⓒ

Test 9 Critical Reasoning

This test is designed to find out how well you are able to evaluate the logic of various kinds of arguments. It is suitable for candidates for junior, middle and senior management jobs over a wide range of industries.

Instructions: The test consists of a passage, which is followed by several statements. Your task is to read the passage and evaluate each statement according to the following rules:

Mark circle A if the statement must be true based on the information in the passage.

Mark circle B if the statement is definitely false given the information in the passage.

Mark circle C if you cannot say whether the statement is true or false without further information.

Base your answers only on the information given in the passage.

Time guideline: There is no official time limit for this test, just work as fast and as accurately as you can.

Indicate your answer each time by filling in completely the appropriate circle in the answer sheet.

Antiques

Forty years ago articles were only considered to be antiques if they were over 100 years old. This made them expensive and it was assumed that collecting was limited to the elite and the rich. Since then TV programmes and specialist magazines have captured public interest. This, and the drop in the age at which an article is considered to be an antique has awoken public demand. In many towns in the UK antique shops and markets have become the focus for collectors, dealers and interested browsers. Some towns, particularly renowned for their antiques shops and markets, attract many foreign visitors, particularly European and American tourists.

1   More antiques shops have opened since the popularity of antique collecting has risen.

2   Before the rise of related TV shows and magazines, antique collecting was a pastime limited to only the privileged in society.

3   Over the last 40 years the definition of what can be classed as an antique has been lowered in terms of age.

Test 9 Answer Sheet

	A	B	C
1	Ⓐ	Ⓑ	Ⓒ
2	Ⓐ	Ⓑ	Ⓒ
3	Ⓐ	Ⓑ	Ⓒ

Test 10 Critical Reasoning

This test is also designed to find out how well you are able to evaluate the logic of various kinds of arguments. It is suitable for candidates for junior, middle and senior management jobs over a wide range of industries.

Instructions: The test consists of a passage, which is followed by several statements. Your task is to read the passage and evaluate each statement according to the following rules:

Mark circle A if the statement must be true based on the information in the passage.

Mark circle B if the statement is definitely false given the information in the passage.

Mark circle C if you cannot say whether the statement is true or false without further information.

Base your answers only on the information given in the passage.

Time guideline: There is no official time limit for this test, just work as fast and as accurately as you can.

Indicate your answer each time by filling in completely the appropriate circle in the answer sheet.

Health Care Workers

Health care workers are at increased risk of both non-fatal and fatal injuries due to a number of factors. Amongst them are both a decrease in medical and mental health care and an increase in the use of hospitals for severely disturbed violent cases whether from drug overdose, severe mental illness, or other types of atypical behaviour. This violence is increasing in severity and frequency in areas such as hospitals, pharmacies and community care facilities and is now a more serious problem than ever before. One solution to this problem would be to limit the early release of the chronically mentally ill from specialist care facilities.

---

1 The proportion of beds made available to those with severe mental illness has increased over recent years.

2 By allowing people who have mental health problems to remain in specialist care for longer, a decrease in the attacks in hospitals might be seen.

3 The increased risk of injury to care workers is wholly due to a decrease in health care and an increase in the hospitalisation of those with mental health problems.

Test 10 Answer Sheet

	A	B	C
1	Ⓐ	Ⓑ	Ⓒ
2	Ⓐ	Ⓑ	Ⓒ
3	Ⓐ	Ⓑ	Ⓒ

Test 11 Verbal Analysis

This test is designed to measure your ability to understand written information, drawing inferences and summarising. It is suitable for candidates for junior, middle and senior management jobs over a wide range of industries.

Instructions: Choose the correct answer to each question by basing your answers on the information contained in the passage and not on general knowledge. Some questions have 2 options, others have 5. For each answer, mark, by filling in completely, the appropriate circle in the answer section.

Time guideline: see how many questions you can answer in 8 minutes.

Accountants have shown how simple it is to inflate profits artificially by manipulating accounting standards, while the stock market demonstrates that such artificial inflation will be followed by natural deflation: many companies have been humbled by falling profits and share prices. Certainly, accounting standards are as much to

5   blame as accountants, but the heart of the problem is that tension between the interests of management and those of shareholders is almost invariably resolved in favour of management. Shareholders notionally have the right to vote against the re-election of auditors, but they never do, and it is the management that signs the cheques. It is desirable for the accounting profession to police itself more effectively

10   and for shareholders to take more seriously their responsibility for the election of auditors. However, neither is likely to happen.

---

1   Which of the following best replaces the word 'notionally' (line 7)?

   A   actually

   B   theoretically

   C   figuratively

   D   legally

   E   naturally.

2   Why is it unlikely according to the passage that the accounting profession will begin policing itself more effectively?

A   The accounting profession has insufficient resources.

B   The management of companies would prevent this.

C   The accounting profession would lose profit.

D   The accounting profession does not want shareholders to become involved in electing auditors.

E   Cannot say.

3   Which **one** of the following summarises the overall message of the passage?

A   Shareholders should become more actively involved in company proceedings than at present.

B   Management should not be more influential than shareholders in the appointment of external advisors.

C   Auditors' activities should not be controlled by the purse but by professional ethics.

D   Manipulation of accounting standards is ultimately undesirable and should be prevented.

E   Inflation and deflation are not always caused by legitimate influences.

4   Can it be inferred from the passage that most companies overstate their profits?

A   Yes

B   No

The government has recently attempted to integrate the environmental clean-up of industry under one umbrella. To minimise environmental damage, the volume of pollutants emitted from a plant has to be authorised by an official pollution control inspectorate.

5   Industry has complained repeatedly about the time and cost of getting operations approved under the new system. The inspectors maintain, however, that industry often has itself to blame for delays as many applications provide insufficient data. Industry has also worried about public access to the information it supplies to get authorisation. Information can only be withheld from public registers on the grounds

10 of commercial confidentiality, if a company can prove it would be disadvantaged by disclosure.

5 For which **two** of the following reasons was the new pollution control system set up?

   A   To provide an integrated approach to pollution control.

   B   To reduce the number of toxins utilised by industry.

   C   To maintain the quantity of contaminants at an acceptable level.

   D   To ensure that each industrial company operates competitively.

   E   To enable applications to be authorised quickly.

6 Is it true according to the passage that obtaining authorisation on operations results in having to divulge confidential information to competitors?

   A   Yes

   B   No

7 Can it be inferred from the passage that industry has not welcomed the introduction of the official pollution control inspectorate?

   A   Yes

   B   No

8 According to the passage, how accurate is the statement, 'There would be no environmental destruction if there were no pollutants.'?

   A   Definitely true

   B   Like to be true

   C   Likely to be untrue

   D   Definitely untrue

   E   Cannot say

Test 11 Answer Sheet

	A	B	C	D	E
1	Ⓐ	Ⓑ	Ⓒ	Ⓓ	Ⓔ
2	Ⓐ	Ⓑ	Ⓒ	Ⓓ	Ⓔ
3	Ⓐ	Ⓑ	Ⓒ	Ⓓ	Ⓔ
4	Ⓐ	Ⓑ			
5	Ⓐ	Ⓑ	Ⓒ	Ⓓ	Ⓔ
6	Ⓐ	Ⓑ			
7	Ⓐ	Ⓑ			
8	Ⓐ	Ⓑ	Ⓒ	Ⓓ	Ⓔ

Answers to verbal reasoning questions

Test 1 Verbal Application

	A	B	C	D	E
1	Ⓐ	Ⓑ	●	Ⓓ	Ⓔ
2	Ⓐ	●	Ⓒ	Ⓓ	Ⓔ
3	Ⓐ	Ⓑ	Ⓒ	●	Ⓔ
4	Ⓐ	Ⓑ	Ⓒ	Ⓓ	●
5	Ⓐ	Ⓑ	●	Ⓓ	Ⓔ
6	Ⓐ	Ⓑ	Ⓒ	Ⓓ	●
7	Ⓐ	Ⓑ	●	Ⓓ	Ⓔ
8	●	Ⓑ	Ⓒ	Ⓓ	Ⓔ

Test 4 Verbal Evaluation

	A	B	C
1	●	Ⓑ	Ⓒ
2	Ⓐ	●	Ⓒ
3	Ⓐ	●	Ⓒ
4	Ⓐ	Ⓑ	●
5	●	Ⓑ	Ⓒ
6	Ⓐ	●	Ⓒ
7	●	Ⓑ	Ⓒ
8	Ⓐ	Ⓑ	●

Test 2 Verbal Evaluation

	A	B	C
1	●	Ⓑ	Ⓒ
2	Ⓐ	●	Ⓒ
3	Ⓐ	Ⓑ	●
4	●	Ⓑ	Ⓒ
5	Ⓐ	Ⓑ	●
6	Ⓐ	●	Ⓒ
7	Ⓐ	●	Ⓒ
8	●	Ⓑ	Ⓒ

Test 5 Verbal Evaluation

	A	B	C
1	Ⓐ	●	Ⓒ
2	Ⓐ	Ⓑ	●
3	●	Ⓑ	Ⓒ
4	Ⓐ	Ⓑ	●
5	●	Ⓑ	Ⓒ
6	●	Ⓑ	Ⓒ
7	Ⓐ	●	Ⓒ
8	Ⓐ	Ⓑ	●

Test 3 Verbal Test

	A	B	C
1	Ⓐ	Ⓑ	●
2	Ⓐ	●	Ⓒ
3	●	Ⓑ	Ⓒ
4	Ⓐ	Ⓑ	●
5	Ⓐ	●	Ⓒ
6	Ⓐ	Ⓑ	●

Test 6 Verbal Evaluation

	A	B	C
1	Ⓐ	●	Ⓒ
2	●	Ⓑ	Ⓒ
3	Ⓐ	Ⓑ	●
4	Ⓐ	Ⓑ	●
5	●	Ⓑ	Ⓒ
6	Ⓐ	●	Ⓒ
7	Ⓐ	Ⓑ	●
8	Ⓐ	Ⓑ	●

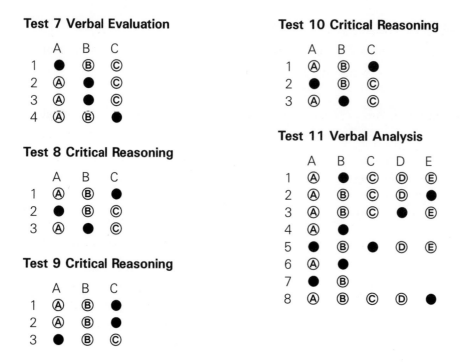

Test 7 Verbal Evaluation

	A	B	C
1	●	Ⓑ	Ⓒ
2	Ⓐ	●	Ⓒ
3	Ⓐ	●	Ⓒ
4	Ⓐ	Ⓑ	●

Test 8 Critical Reasoning

	A	B	C
1	Ⓐ	Ⓑ	●
2	●	Ⓑ	Ⓒ
3	Ⓐ	●	Ⓒ

Test 9 Critical Reasoning

	A	B	C
1	Ⓐ	Ⓑ	●
2	Ⓐ	Ⓑ	●
3	●	Ⓑ	Ⓒ

Test 10 Critical Reasoning

	A	B	C
1	Ⓐ	Ⓑ	●
2	●	Ⓑ	Ⓒ
3	Ⓐ	●	Ⓒ

Test 11 Verbal Analysis

	A	B	C	D	E
1	Ⓐ	●	Ⓒ	Ⓓ	Ⓔ
2	Ⓐ	Ⓑ	Ⓒ	Ⓓ	●
3	Ⓐ	Ⓑ	Ⓒ	●	Ⓔ
4	Ⓐ	●			
5	●	Ⓑ	●	Ⓓ	Ⓔ
6	Ⓐ	●			
7	●	Ⓑ			
8	Ⓐ	Ⓑ	Ⓒ	Ⓓ	●

Verbal and critical reasoning tests – how to improve your performance

◆ Read books and quality newspapers.

◆ Whenever you are uncertain how to spell a particular word, look it up. The more you do this, the more your spelling will improve. Using a computer spell-check regularly will also help considerably.

◆ Try verbal problem-solving exercises, such as crosswords.

◆ For managerial positions, also read reports and business journals, especially those concerning the industry to which you are applying. It's important that you become conversant with the vocabulary and jargon of the industry to which you are applying.

◆ For managerial jobs in technical fields, also consider reading technical manuals and instruction books. It always helps to know what you're talking about!

◆ When attempting verbal tests that test your spelling your intuitive first guess is likely to be the correct one. If you spend too long staring at the words, they'll all look wrong – even the ones which are correctly spelt.

◆ In **critical reasoning tests**, always read the passage thoroughly. Don't skip through sections, or scan the text at high speed. Reading with understanding requires concentrated effort – not an easy thing to do however good your reading skills. Re-read anything of which you are unsure.

◆ Also study the questions themselves very carefully to ensure you understand exactly what it is you are being asked. Sometimes critical reasoning questions can appear a little ambiguous at first glance.

◆ Consider the answer choices and quickly eliminate any you know to be incorrect. Then concentrate your energies on deciding between the most likely possibilities.

◆ Think carefully before selecting an answer which includes words like *always*, *never*, *true*, *false*, *none* and *all*. These words leave no room for manoeuvre or any exception whatsoever.

◆ Answer the questions using only the given information. Don't let prior knowledge or your opinion on the subject matter influence you. Only your ability to understand and make logical deductions *from the passage* is being tested.

◆ Verbal reasoning tests demand a high level of concentration, so treat yourself to a break every now and then. Sit up straight, shut your eyes and take a few deep breaths, just for 20 seconds or so. This will calm you down, relax your back and give your eyes and brain a well deserved rest.

◆ If you really feel a question is misleading, ambiguous, or simply wrong, make an educated guess and move on. Mistakes do crop up occasionally – occupational psychologists are only human after all!

CHAPTER FIVE

Numerical Reasoning

Numerical reasoning tests are multiple-choice psychometric tests which are used as part of the selection procedure for jobs with any element of figure work or data analysis. This includes a wide range of jobs, such as those dealing with money, buying, administration, IT, engineering, statistics, analytical science and, of course, management.

Numerical reasoning questions can be presented in a variety of different ways, including:

* basic maths
* sequences (usually numbers but can also be letters of the alphabet)
* number problems
* numerical estimation problems
* data interpretation using tables, graphs and diagrams.

You will often come across the simpler type of maths test at the beginning of the recruitment process, either as part of the online testing or at assessment event. These tests usually include basic maths, sequences, straightforward number problems and perhaps a little numerical estimation thrown in for good measure. Assuming you are fairly numerate, you should sail through these tests with ease. After that, expect things to get more difficult.

For higher-level jobs at managerial level your ability to get to grips with basic arithmetic is taken as read. Instead, your ability to analyse, interpret and manipulate complex numerical data is examined, for obvious reasons. Being able to understand, consider and logically evaluate complex information is an absolutely essential qualification for virtually all managerial positions (not just jobs in finance).

These higher-level numerical reasoning tests are almost always presented in the form of graphs, tables, charts and diagrams, usually worded to incorporate some sort of business scenario or problem.

Note: Management-level numerical reasoning tests can also be referred to as *critical numerical reasoning tests,* or *data analysis exercises.*

Calculators are often allowed, simply because it's your analytical skills, rather than your computational prowess that are being tested.

Having said that, you won't be able to tackle any of these higher-level tests without a sound grasp of the basics, so make sure you are absolutely familiar and confident with all of the following:

✓ addition
✓ subtraction
✓ multiplication
✓ division
✓ decimal numbers
✓ fractions
✓ percentages.

In common with all other ability-type psychometric tests, all numerical reasoning tests are strictly timed, with questions having *one, and only one correct answer* (although occasionally you will come across a question that requires *two* answers).

In this chapter

In this chapter there are 9 different management-level numerical psychometric tests for you to try. In the introduction to each test I have indicated the job level and specific skills being tested.

At the very end of the chapter there is section entitled **Numerical reasoning tests – how to improve your performance** which includes hints and tips to help you do just that across the whole range of numerical tests. If you have a problem with any of the questions then hopefully the advice contained in this section will get you back on track. Remember however that all of us have strengths and weaknesses, and everyone will have some difficulty with some of the tests in this book.

Note: do not use a calculator unless specifically instructed to.

Test 12 Numerical Reasoning

This test measures your ability to solve short numerical problems quickly – an essential skill for managers. It is suitable for candidates for junior, middle and senior management jobs over a wide range of industries.

Instructions: Choose the correct answer from the 5 options given for each question and mark, by filling in completely, the appropriate circle in the answer section at the end of the test. *You may use a calculator.*

Time guideline: see how many questions you can answer in 7 minutes.

1	If a maintenance contract costs £87 per month and a technician call-out not under a maintenance contract £325, now many calls-outs per year would make the contract worthwhile?				
	A	B	C	D	E
	4	5	6	7	8

2	If every 250 bottles of bleach require 16.25 litres of solvent to produce, how much solvent is required to produce 6,500 bottles of bleach?				
	A	B	C	D	E
	42.3 litres	100.0 litres	121.9 litres	422.5 litres	1,219.0 litres

3	Last year's sales target was £265,000. This year's is £328,000. By what percentage has this year's sales target increased over last year's?				
	A	B	C	D	E
	17%	29%	43%	81%	none of these

4 | A total of 5,200 analyses last month required 17,300 hours of computer time. Approximately how much computer time would be required to perform an additional 300 analyses if all other factors remain unchanged?

A	B	C	D	E
330 hours	540 hours	660 hours	940 hours	1,000 hours

5 | A batch of shampoo requires 510 litres of herbal extracts and 13,400 litres of water. What is the approximate ratio of water to herbal exctracts?

A	B	C	D	E
26:1	3.8:1	1:26	1:38	1:260

Branch	Profit		
	Year 1	Year 2	Year 3
A	£4.6m	£4.8m	£4.7m
B	£2.8m	£2.9m	£2.5m
C	£6.1m	£6.4m	£6.6m

6 | How many times over the period did Branches A, B or C experience a reduction in profit?

A	B	C	D	E
0	1	2	3	4

7 | By what percentage did the total profit made by Branches A, B and C increase from Year 1 to Year 3?

A	B	C	D	E
2.0%	2.2%	20.0%	22.0%	102.0%

8 | Temporary staff are paid £6.00 per hour. If 47 hours were worked last week by each of 7 temporary staff, what was the total bill?

A	B	C	D	E
£197	£282	£329	£846	£1,974

8 | If 625kg of fruit are required to produce 200 jars of jam, approximately how much fruit is required to produce 450 jars of jam?

A	B	C	D	E
144kg	531kg	864kg	1,270kg	1,406kg

10 | A survey carried out on 1,500 people showed that 37% liked a new product, while 32% were indifferent. If the rest said they disliked the produce, how many people were in this category?

A	B	C	D	E
48	237	465	945	1,020

11 | In an average week, the computer is down for 2.75 hours. Lost revenue per hour is £425,000. What is the approximate total revenue lost in a 52 week year?

A	B	C	D	E
£0.23m	£8.04m	£12.01m	£47.26m	£60.78m

12	The Operating Profit last year was £7.75m. If there is an increase this year of 13%, what will this year's Operating Profit be?

A	B	C	D	E
£7,945,000	£8,126,800	£8,346,200	£8,757,500	none of these

13	Of a total of 225 employees, 32% are female. 89% of female employees are between the ages of 20 and 35. How many employees are females between the ages of 20 and 35?

A	B	C	D	E
12	58	64	89	201

14	If a department makes a profit of 30% on a turnover of £85,000, what percentage profit can be expected if overheads increase by £10,000 but other factors remain unchanged?

A	B	C	D	E
5%	10%	14%	18%	25%

Test 12 Answer Sheet

	A	B	C	D	E
1	Ⓐ	Ⓑ	Ⓒ	Ⓓ	Ⓔ
2	Ⓐ	Ⓑ	Ⓒ	Ⓓ	Ⓔ
3	Ⓐ	Ⓑ	Ⓒ	Ⓓ	Ⓔ
4	Ⓐ	Ⓑ	Ⓒ	Ⓓ	Ⓔ
5	Ⓐ	Ⓑ	Ⓒ	Ⓓ	Ⓔ
6	Ⓐ	Ⓑ	Ⓒ	Ⓓ	Ⓔ
7	Ⓐ	Ⓑ	Ⓒ	Ⓓ	Ⓔ
8	Ⓐ	Ⓑ	Ⓒ	Ⓓ	Ⓔ
9	Ⓐ	Ⓑ	Ⓒ	Ⓓ	Ⓔ
10	Ⓐ	Ⓑ	Ⓒ	Ⓓ	Ⓔ
11	Ⓐ	Ⓑ	Ⓒ	Ⓓ	Ⓔ
12	Ⓐ	Ⓑ	Ⓒ	Ⓓ	Ⓔ
13	Ⓐ	Ⓑ	Ⓒ	Ⓓ	Ⓔ
14	Ⓐ	Ⓑ	Ⓒ	Ⓓ	Ⓔ

Test 13 Interpreting Data

This test measures your ability to understand facts and figures in statistical tables and make logical deductions from the given information. Certainly, the ability to interpret data from a variety of different sources such as tables, graphs and charts is a common requirement in many managerial and professional jobs.

This type of test is often used to select candidates for administrative and supervisory jobs, as well as junior managers and management trainees, and any job involving analysis or decision-making based on numerical facts.

Instructions: For each question, indicate your answer by filling in completely the appropriate circle on the answer sheet. *Do not use a calculator. You may use rough paper for your workings-out.*

Time guideline: There is no official time guideline for this practice test. However, try to work through the questions as quickly as you can. Remember that accuracy is equally important.

Newspaper Readership				
	Readership (millions)		Percentage of Adults Reading each Paper in 1990	
Daily Newspapers	1981	1990	Males	Females
The Daily Chronicle	3.6	2.9	7	6
Daily News	13.8	9.3	24	18
The Tribune	1.1	1.4	4	3
The Herald	8.5	12.7	30	23
Daily Echo	4.8	4.9	10	12

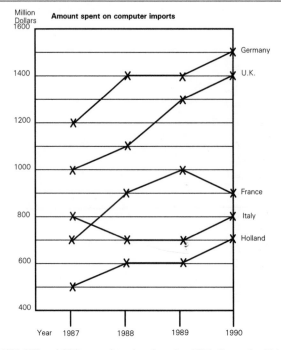

1   Which newspaper was read by a higher percentage of females than males in 1990?

A	B	C	D	E
The Tribune	The Herald	Daily News	Daily Echo	The Daily Chronicle

2   In 1989, how much more than Italy did Germany spend on computer imports?

A	B	C	D	E
650 million	700 million	750 million	800 million	850 million

3   What was the combined readership of the Daily Chronicle, Echo and Tribune in 1981?

A	B	C	D	E
10.6	8.4	9.5	12.2	7.8

4   If the amount spent on computer imports into the U.K. in 1991 was 20% lower than in 1990, what was spent in 1991?

A	B	C	D	E
£1080	£1120	£1160	£1220	£1300

5   Which newspaper showed the largest change in female readership between 1981 and 1990?

A	B	C	D	E
Daily Echo	The Tribune	The Herald	The Daily Chronicle	Cannot Say

6   Which countries experienced a drop in the value of computers imported from one year to the next?

A	B	C	D	E
France and Italy	France and Holland	Holland and Italy	U.K. and Holland	Italy and U.K.

Test 13 Answer Sheet

	A	B	C	D	E
1	Ⓐ	Ⓑ	Ⓒ	Ⓓ	Ⓔ
2	Ⓐ	Ⓑ	Ⓒ	Ⓓ	Ⓔ
3	Ⓐ	Ⓑ	Ⓒ	Ⓓ	Ⓔ
4	Ⓐ	Ⓑ	Ⓒ	Ⓓ	Ⓔ
5	Ⓐ	Ⓑ	Ⓒ	Ⓓ	Ⓔ
6	Ⓐ	Ⓑ	Ⓒ	Ⓓ	Ⓔ

Test 14 Numerical Test

This test measures your ability to understand facts and figures in statistical tables and make logical deductions from the given information. The ability to interpret data from a variety of different sources such as tables, graphs and charts is a common requirement in many managerial and professional jobs.

   This type of test is used in the selection of graduates, managers and supervisors over a wide range of industries.

Instructions: For each question you are given either five or ten options from which to choose. One, and only one of the answers is correct in each case. Indicate your answer by filling in completely the appropriate circle on the answer sheet. Please note that for questions which have 10 options you may have to fill in more than one circle to indicate your answer. *Some organisations allow the use of a calculator for this test, others do not. Therefore I suggest you try to manage without.*

Time guideline: There is no official time guideline. However work as quickly as you can. *You may use rough paper for your workings-out.*

Statistical tables

Population Structure 1985

	Population at start of year (millions)	Live Births per 1,000 population (Jan-Dec)	Deaths per 1,000 population (Jan-Dec)	Percentage of population at start of year aged under 15	60 or over
UK	56.6	13.3	11.8	19	21
France	55.2	13.9	10.0	21	19
Italy	57.1	10.1	9.5	19	19
West Germany	61.0	9.6	11.5	15	20
Spain	38.6	12.1	7.7	23	17

Production of 15mm Buttons, July–December

Sales price standard quality buttons – £5.70 per 100.
Sales price sub-standard buttons – £2.85 per 100.

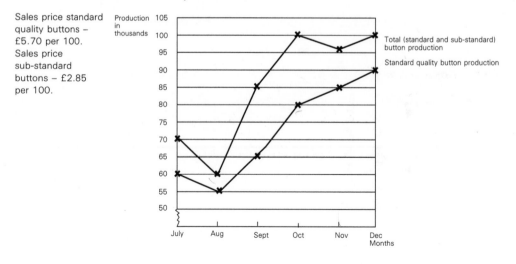

Total (standard and sub-standard) button production

Standard quality button production

1 Which country had the highest number of people aged 60 or over at the start of 1985?

A	B	C	D	E
UK	France	Italy	W. Germany	Spain

2 What percentage of the total 15mm button production was classed as sub-standard in September?

A	B	C	D	E
10.5%	13%	15%	17.5%	20%

AB	AC	AD	AE	BC
23.5%	25%	27.5%	28%	30.5%

3 How many live births occurred in 1985 in Spain and Italy together (to the nearest 1,000)?

A	B	C	D	E
104,000	840,000	1,044,000	8,400,000	10,440,000

4 What was the net effect on the UK population of the live birth and death rates in 1985?

A	B	C	D	E
Decrease of 66,700	Increase of 84,900	Increase of 85,270	Increase of 742,780	Cannot say

5 By how much did the total sales value of November's button production vary from October's?

A	B	C	D	E
£28.50 (Decrease)	£142.40 (Decrease)	£285.00 (Increase)	£427.50 (Decrease)	No change

6 What was the loss in potential sales revenue attributable to the production of sub-standard (as opposed to standard) buttons over the 6 month period?

A	B	C	D	E
£213.75	£427.50	£2,137.50	£2,280.00	£4,275.00

Test 14 Answer Sheet

	A	B	C	D	E
1	Ⓐ	Ⓑ	Ⓒ	Ⓓ	Ⓔ
2	Ⓐ	Ⓑ	Ⓒ	Ⓓ	Ⓔ
3	Ⓐ	Ⓑ	Ⓒ	Ⓓ	Ⓔ
4	Ⓐ	Ⓑ	Ⓒ	Ⓓ	Ⓔ
5	Ⓐ	Ⓑ	Ⓒ	Ⓓ	Ⓔ
6	Ⓐ	Ⓑ	Ⓒ	Ⓓ	Ⓔ

Test 15 Numerical Interpretation

In this test you will be using facts and figures presented in various tables to answer questions designed to assess your ability to reason with data – a common requirement of many managerial and professional jobs. This type of test is often used to select candidates for jobs in sales and customer contact areas at supervisory and junior management level, and for jobs involving analysis or decision-making based on numerical facts.

Instructions: Using the information in the table and pie chart, answer each question by filling in completely the appropriate circle on the answer sheet. Remember that each question has one, and only one, correct answer. *You may use a calculator.*

Time guideline: See how many questions you can answer in 5 minutes.

TELEPHONE CALLS RECEIVED BY CUSTOMER SERVICES THIS MONTH				
Person taking call	Number of product enquiries	Number of complaints	Number of accounts queries	Total number of calls
Jo	155	6	6	167
Mark	310	2	10	322
Michelle	205	0	47	252
Susan	112	14	25	151
Tony	370	8	35	413

COST OF PROMOTIONAL ACTIVITIES IN LAST FINANCIAL YEAR

Total cost over year: £80,000

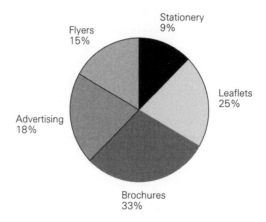

Stationery 9%
Flyers 15%
Leaflets 25%
Advertising 18%
Brochures 33%

1   How many product enquiries were received this month?

A	B	C	D	E
1,142	1,152	1,182	1,232	1,292

2   If each complaint call lasted for an average of 12 mins, how much time was spent dealing with complaint calls?

A	B	C	D	E
5 hours 12 mins	5 hours 24 mins	5 hours 36 mins	5 hours 48 mins	6 hours

3   Two-thirds of complaining customers received a £15 voucher and the rest received a £50 voucher. What was the total value of these vouchers?

A	B	C	D	E
£500	£760	£800	£1,010	£1,150

4   How much money was spent on promotional stationery in the last financial year?

A	B	C	D	E
£4,900	£5,300	£6,800	£7,200	£7,400

5   If 50,000 brochures were printed, what was the approximate cost per brochure?

A	B	C	D	E
26p	44p	53p	62p	78p

6   If the average cost of printing a flyer is 4p, how many were printed in the last financial year?

A	B	C	D	E
200,000	300,000	400,000	600,000	900,000

Test 15 Answer Sheet

	A	B	C	D	E
1	Ⓐ	Ⓑ	Ⓒ	Ⓓ	Ⓔ
2	Ⓐ	Ⓑ	Ⓒ	Ⓓ	Ⓔ
3	Ⓐ	Ⓑ	Ⓒ	Ⓓ	Ⓔ
4	Ⓐ	Ⓑ	Ⓒ	Ⓓ	Ⓔ
5	Ⓐ	Ⓑ	Ⓒ	Ⓓ	Ⓔ
6	Ⓐ	Ⓑ	Ⓒ	Ⓓ	Ⓔ

Test 16 Interpreting Numerical Data

The ability to interpret, analyse and evaluate numerical or statistical data is a common requirement for many management jobs, especially those involving any decision-making based on numerical facts.

Instructions: In this test you will be using facts and figures presented in a diagram to answer a range of questions. In each question you are given five alternative answers to choose from. Fill in completely the appropriate circle on the answer sheet. One and only one of the alternatives is correct in each case.
You may use rough paper and a pencil for working out your answers, but *not a calculator*.

Time guideline: Try to answer all the questions in 4 minutes.

Full-time employment destinations of women leaving university

TOTAL = 6,500

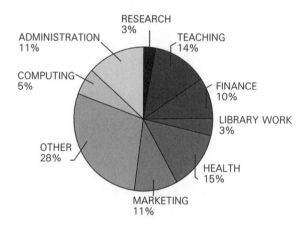

1   What percentage of women leaving university went into finance and administration?

A	B	C	D	E
11%	19%	22%	21%	31%

2   Which one area of employment is least popular with female university leavers?

A	B	C	D	E
Computing	Library Work	Marketing	Research	Cannot say

3 Which area of work was most frequently chosen by women leaving university?

A	B	C	D	E
Administration	Finance	Health	Sales	Teaching

4 Into which two areas of employment did a combined 19% of female university leavers go?

A	B	C	D	E
Administration and Computing	Health and Research	Marketing and Administration	Teaching and Computing	Teaching and Library

5 How many women went into teaching when they left university?

A	B	C	D	E
140	650	870	910	None of these

6 How many more women went into computing than research?

A	B	C	D	E
120	135	195	325	None of these

7 How many women went into computing and administration?

A	B	C	D	E
940	1,040	1,100	1,140	None of these

8 24% of female university leavers go into ...

A	B	C	D	E
Finance, Research and Administration	Finance, Teaching and Research	Health, Computing and Research	Marketing, Finance and Computing	Teaching, Research and Administration

Test 16 Answer Sheet

	A	B	C	D	E
1	Ⓐ	Ⓑ	Ⓒ	Ⓓ	Ⓔ
2	Ⓐ	Ⓑ	Ⓒ	Ⓓ	Ⓔ
3	Ⓐ	Ⓑ	Ⓒ	Ⓓ	Ⓔ
4	Ⓐ	Ⓑ	Ⓒ	Ⓓ	Ⓔ
5	Ⓐ	Ⓑ	Ⓒ	Ⓓ	Ⓔ
6	Ⓐ	Ⓑ	Ⓒ	Ⓓ	Ⓔ
7	Ⓐ	Ⓑ	Ⓒ	Ⓓ	Ⓔ
8	Ⓐ	Ⓑ	Ⓒ	Ⓓ	Ⓔ

Test 17 Interpreting Numerical Data

The ability to interpret, analyse and evaluate numerical or statistical data is a common requirement for many management jobs, especially those involving any decision-making based on numerical facts.

Instructions: In this test you will be using facts and figures presented in a graph to answer a range of questions. In each question you are given five alternative answers to choose from. Fill in completely the appropriate circle on the answer sheet. One and only one of the alternatives is correct in each case.
You may use rough paper and a pencil for working out your answers, but *not a calculator*.

Time guideline: Try to answer all the questions in 4 minutes.

Merchandise, coal and liquid lifted (carried) by inland waterways

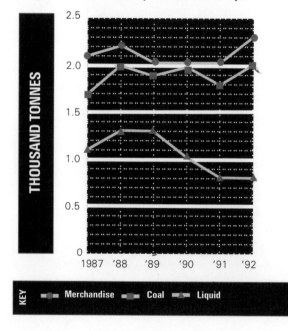

1 How many thousand tonnes of liquids were lifted in 1989?

A	B	C	D	E
1.3	1.5	1.9	2.00	None of these

2 How much more coal was lifted in 1992 than in 1987? (Answer choices are given in thousand tonnes.)

A	B	C	D	E
0.1	0.2	0.3	1.3	2.0

3 How many thousand tonnes of merchandise and liquids were lifted in 1991?

A	B	C	D	E
2.2	2.8	2.9	3.00	1.9

4 In which year was most merchandise carried?

A	B	C	D	E
1988	1990	1991	1992	1989

5 In 1988 how much more merchandise than liquids was lifted? (Answer choices are given in thousand tonnes.)

A	B	C	D	E
0.2	0.9	1.00	1.1	2.2

6 How much more liquid was carried in 1989 than in 1992? (Answer choices are given in thousand tonnes.)

A	B	C	D	E
0.5	0.8	1.3	1.5	1.8

7 In which year was an equal tonnage of merchandise and coal carried?

A	B	C	D	E
1987	1988	1990	1991	1992

Test 17 Answer Sheet

	A	B	C	D	E
1	Ⓐ	Ⓑ	Ⓒ	Ⓓ	Ⓔ
2	Ⓐ	Ⓑ	Ⓒ	Ⓓ	Ⓔ
3	Ⓐ	Ⓑ	Ⓒ	Ⓓ	Ⓔ
4	Ⓐ	Ⓑ	Ⓒ	Ⓓ	Ⓔ
5	Ⓐ	Ⓑ	Ⓒ	Ⓓ	Ⓔ
6	Ⓐ	Ⓑ	Ⓒ	Ⓓ	Ⓔ
7	Ⓐ	Ⓑ	Ⓒ	Ⓓ	Ⓔ

Test 18 Interpreting Numerical Data

The ability to interpret, analyse and evaluate numerical or statistical data is a common requirement for many management jobs, especially those involving any decision-making based on numerical facts.

Instructions: In this test you will be using facts and figures presented in a table to answer a range of questions. In each question you are given five alternative answers to choose from. Fill in completely the appropriate circle on the answer sheet. One and only one of the alternatives is correct in each case.
You may use rough paper and a pencil for working out your answers, but *not a calculator*.

Time guideline: Try to answer all the questions in 4 minutes.

Expenditure per pupil (£)

	PRIMARY SCHOOLS	
	London Authorities	Other Authorities
Staff	774	565
Premises	134	85
Books and equipment	34	21
Other	6	7

	SECONDARY SCHOOLS	
	London Authorities	Other Authorities
Staff	1088	797
Premises	184	137
Books and equipment	61	36
Other	24	15

1 How much more per pupil do London authorities spend on staff in secondary schools than in primary schools?

A	B	C	D	E
£209	£219	£232	£291	£314

2 How much more than 'other' authorities do London authorities spend per secondary pupil on premises?

A	B	C	D	E
£39	£47	£184	£137	£291

3   What is the total cost to London authorities per secondary school pupil?

A	B	C	D	E
£688	£948	£985	£1,357	£1,427

4   On what do 'other' authorities spend 13.8% of their total outlay per primary school pupil?

A	B	C	D	E
Books and Equipment	Premises	Staff	Other	Cannot say

5   What is the total expenditure for a primary school in London with 320 pupils?

A	B	C	D	E
£300,360	£303,360	£330,306	£330,360	£360,303

6   What is the difference in total cost to London authorities between one secondary pupil and one primary pupil?

A	B	C	D	E
£260	£314	£409	£948	None of these

7   Approximately what proportion of the total amount spent per primary pupil by 'other' authorities is on books and equipment?

A	B	C	D	E
1%	3%	10%	12%	17%

Test 18 Answer Sheet

	A	B	C	D	E
1	Ⓐ	Ⓑ	Ⓒ	Ⓓ	Ⓔ
2	Ⓐ	Ⓑ	Ⓒ	Ⓓ	Ⓔ
3	Ⓐ	Ⓑ	Ⓒ	Ⓓ	Ⓔ
4	Ⓐ	Ⓑ	Ⓒ	Ⓓ	Ⓔ
5	Ⓐ	Ⓑ	Ⓒ	Ⓓ	Ⓔ
6	Ⓐ	Ⓑ	Ⓒ	Ⓓ	Ⓔ
7	Ⓐ	Ⓑ	Ⓒ	Ⓓ	Ⓔ

Test 19 Numerical Analysis

This test measures your ability to interpret and utilise business-related numerical data – an essential skill for managers. It is suitable for candidates for junior, middle and senior management jobs over a wide range of industries.

Instructions: Choose the correct answer from the 5 options given for each question by using the data provided and mark, by filling in completely, the appropriate circle in the answer section. You will only need to refer to the set of information given above every four questions. *You may use a calculator.*

Time guideline: See how many questions you can answer in 8 minutes.

STAFF PROFILE, YEAR 1

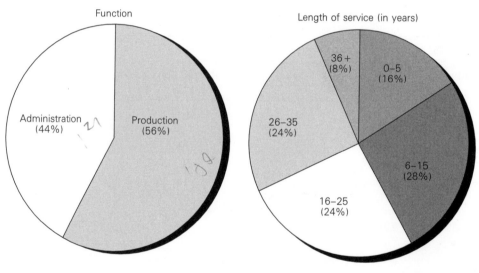

Total number of staff = 275

1	How many more production staff are there than administrative staff?				
	A 12	B 27	C 33	D 110	E cannot say

2	How many administrative staff have served between 10 and 20 years?				
	A 31	B 57	C 72	D 89	E cannot say

3	How many administrative staff are there in the 26 to 35 years' service group, if the proportion of production staff and administration staff is the same for this group as for the overall group?				
	A 11	B 29	C 37	D 49	E 52

4	If half of the 0 to 5 years' service group and all of the 36+ years' service group are production staff, how many production staff are there altogether in the other groups?				
	A 110	B 132	C 164	D 231	E cannot say

SALES FIGURES – YEARS 1 TO 3		Sales (£1,000s)		
		Year 1	Year 2	Year 3
Product group	A	1,420	1,560	1,610
	B	2,670	2,940	2,880
	C	4,100	3,690	3,140
	D	2,360	2,830	3,120
	E	930	1,040	860

SALES DEPARTMENT – STAFF NUMBERS, YEARS 1 to 3

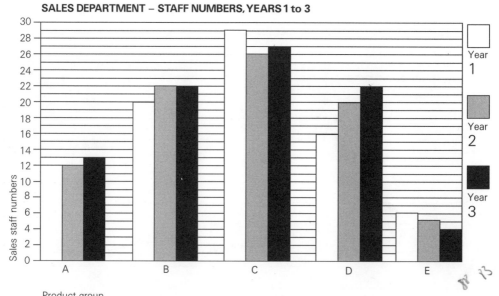

5 | By what percentage did total sales staff numbers change from Year 1 to Year 3?

A	B	C	D	E
2.4%	3.5%	4.8%	6.0%	9.4%

6 | Which product group achieved the best sales results per sales person in Year 2?

A	B	C	D	E
Product Group A	Product Group B	Product Group C	Product Group D	Product Group E

7 | Which product group's sales figures for Years 1 to 3 show the closest trend to its sales staff numbers over the same period?

A	B	C	D	E
Product Group A	Product Group B	Product Group C	Product Group D	Product Group E

8 | If there are 7 additional sales staff in Year 3, and the average sales per person remains constant, how much greater would the total sales for Year 3 be?

A	B	C	D	E
£12,500	£855,500	£923,500	£1,253,400	cannot say

Test 19 Answer Sheet

	A	B	C	D	E
1	Ⓐ	Ⓑ	Ⓒ	Ⓓ	Ⓔ
2	Ⓐ	Ⓑ	Ⓒ	Ⓓ	Ⓔ
3	Ⓐ	Ⓑ	Ⓒ	Ⓓ	Ⓔ
4	Ⓐ	Ⓑ	Ⓒ	Ⓓ	Ⓔ
5	Ⓐ	Ⓑ	Ⓒ	Ⓓ	Ⓔ
6	Ⓐ	Ⓑ	Ⓒ	Ⓓ	Ⓔ
7	Ⓐ	Ⓑ	Ⓒ	Ⓓ	Ⓔ
8	Ⓐ	Ⓑ	Ⓒ	Ⓓ	Ⓔ

Test 20 Numerical Critical Reasoning

Numerical critical reasoning tests measure the ability to make correct decisions or inferences from numerical data. This type of test is used in the selection, development and promotion of work-experienced managements and professional staff across a wide range of job functions and industry sectors.

Instructions: Choose the correct answer from the 5 options given for each question, filling in completely the appropriate circle on the answer sheet which appears on the last page of this test. *You may use a calculator.*

Time guideline: There is no official time guideline for this test, however try to work as quickly and accurately as you can.

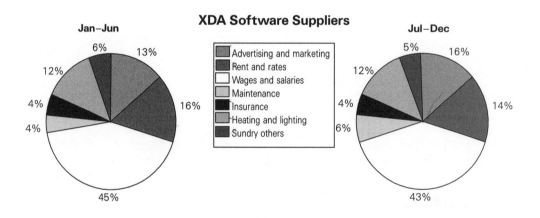

Test 20 © SHL Group plc 2005. SHL and OPQ are registered trademarks of SHL Group plc which are registered in the United Kingdom and other countries.

1   If the 'Wages and salaries' cost was £814,995 in the first half of the year, and if the total expenditure increased by 10% in the second half of the year, what would the 'Wages and salaries' expenditure be in the second half of the year?

A	B	C	D	E
£778,773	£847,595	£856,650	£880,195	£896,494

2   If 'Heating and lighting' costs had been reduced by 10% in the second half of the year, by how much would this have reduced total expenditure over the whole year?

A	B	C	D	E
5%	10%	15%	20%	Cannot say

3   Which two overheads generated a smaller proportion of expenditure costs in the second half of the year (Jul–Dec) than 'Rent and rates' did in the first half of the year (Jan–Jun)?

A	B	C	D	E
'Heating and lighting' and 'Sundry others'	'Maintenance' and 'Sundry others'	'Advertising and marketing' and 'Rent and rates'	'Insurance' and 'Heating' and lighting'	'Rent and rates' and 'Maintenance'

Sectoral Employment Trends			
	Region 1	Region 2	Combined
Food and drink	27%	23%	25%
Clothing and textiles	11%	4%	7%
Paper and printing	10%	8%	9%
Non-metallic minerals	7%	7%	7%
Metals and engineering	20%	21%	20%
Financial services	5%	17%	12%
Other sectors	20%	20%	20%
	100%	100%	100%

4 If 3,300 people work in clothing and textiles in Region 1, how many people work in financial services in the same region?

A	B	C	D	E
1,100	1,300	1,400	1,500	1,650

5 If 2,700 people are employed in non-metallic minerals in Region 1, what is the percentage difference between the number of people employed in food and drink and the number of people employed in financial services in the same region?

A	B	C	D	E
12%	22%	32%	40%	Cannot say

Hotel Alpenblick – double bedroom prices				
	1–2 nights	3–5 nights	6–7 nights	8 nights or more
Low season	€80.00	€70.00	€60.00	€50.00
High season	€128.00	€112.00	€96.00	€80.00

Prices are per room per night

6 A couple received a bill of €280 in total for their stay in Hotel Alpenblick, how many nights and in which season did they stay?

A	B	C	D	E
2 nights, high season	3 nights, low season	4 nights, high season	4 nights, low season	6 nights, low season

7 By what percentage would the price increase if someone decided to book a double bedroom for 6 nights instead of 5 nights in low season?

A	B	C	D	E
3%	7%	11%	16%	20%

8 If a booking was made for 1 double bedroom for 10 nights, of which 2 nights fall into the high season, what would the total price of this booking be?

A	B	C	D	E
€400	€500	€560	€650	€800

Test 20 Answer Sheet

	A	B	C	D	E
1	Ⓐ	Ⓑ	Ⓒ	Ⓓ	Ⓔ
2	Ⓐ	Ⓑ	Ⓒ	Ⓓ	Ⓔ
3	Ⓐ	Ⓑ	Ⓒ	Ⓓ	Ⓔ
4	Ⓐ	Ⓑ	Ⓒ	Ⓓ	Ⓔ
5	Ⓐ	Ⓑ	Ⓒ	Ⓓ	Ⓔ
6	Ⓐ	Ⓑ	Ⓒ	Ⓓ	Ⓔ
7	Ⓐ	Ⓑ	Ⓒ	Ⓓ	Ⓔ
8	Ⓐ	Ⓑ	Ⓒ	Ⓓ	Ⓔ

Answers to numerical reasoning tests

Test 12 Numerical Reasoning

	A	B	C	D	E
1	●	B	C	D	E
2	A	B	C	●	E
3	A	B	C	D	●
4	A	B	C	D	●
5	●	B	C	D	E
6	A	B	●	D	E
7	A	●	C	D	E
8	A	B	C	D	●
9	A	B	C	D	●
10	A	B	●	D	E
11	A	B	C	D	E
12	A	B	C	●	E
13	A	B	●	D	E
14	A	B	C	●	E

Test 13 Interpreting Data

	A	B	C	D	E
1	A	B	C	●	E
2	A	●	C	D	E
3	A	B	●	D	E
4	A	●	C	D	E
5	A	B	C	D	●
6	●	B	C	D	E

Test 14 Numerical Test

	A	B	C	D	E
1	A	B	C	●	E
2	●	●	C	D	E
3	A	B	●	D	E
4	A	●	C	D	E
5	A	B	C	D	●
6	A	B	●	D	E

Test 15 Interpreting Numerical Data

	A	B	C	D	E
1	A	●	C	D	E
2	A	B	C	D	●
3	A	B	●	D	E
4	A	B	C	●	E
5	A	B	●	D	E
6	A	●	C	D	E

Test 16 Interpreting Numerical Data

	A	B	C	D	E
1	A	B	C	●	E
2	A	B	C	D	●
3	A	B	●	D	E
4	A	B	C	●	E
5	A	B	C	●	E
6	A	B	C	D	●
7	A	●	C	D	E
8	●	B	C	D	E

Test 17 Interpreting Numerical Data

	A	B	C	D	E
1	●	B	C	D	E
2	A	B	●	D	E
3	A	●	C	D	E
4	A	B	C	●	E
5	A	●	C	D	E
6	A	B	●	D	E
7	A	B	●	D	E

Test 18 Interpreting Numerical Data

	A	B	C	D	E
1	A	B	C	D	●
2	A	●	C	D	E
3	A	B	C	●	E
4	A	●	C	D	E
5	A	●	C	D	E
6	A	B	●	D	E
7	A	●	C	D	E

Test 19 Numerical Analysis

	A	B	C	D	E
1	Ⓐ	Ⓑ	●	Ⓓ	Ⓔ
2	Ⓐ	Ⓑ	Ⓒ	Ⓓ	●
3	Ⓐ	●	Ⓒ	Ⓓ	Ⓔ
4	●	Ⓑ	Ⓒ	Ⓓ	Ⓔ
5	Ⓐ	Ⓑ	Ⓒ	●	Ⓔ
6	Ⓐ	Ⓑ	Ⓒ	Ⓓ	●
7	Ⓐ	Ⓑ	Ⓒ	●	Ⓔ
8	Ⓐ	Ⓑ	●	Ⓓ	Ⓔ

Test 20 Numerical Critical Reasoning

	A	B	C	D	E
1	Ⓐ	Ⓑ	●	Ⓓ	Ⓔ
2	Ⓐ	Ⓑ	Ⓒ	Ⓓ	●
3	Ⓐ	●	Ⓒ	Ⓓ	Ⓔ
4	Ⓐ	Ⓑ	Ⓒ	●	Ⓔ
5	Ⓐ	●	Ⓒ	Ⓓ	Ⓔ
6	Ⓐ	Ⓑ	Ⓒ	●	Ⓔ
7	●	Ⓑ	Ⓒ	Ⓓ	Ⓔ
8	Ⓐ	Ⓑ	●	Ⓓ	Ⓔ

Numerical tests – how to improve your performance

However numerical reasoning questions are presented, and at whatever level, you really do need a sound understanding of the following basic maths skills:

✓ addition
✓ subtraction
✓ multiplication
✓ division
✓ decimal numbers
✓ fractions
✓ percentages
✓ times tables – learn these by heart.

This is essential, especially for questions which require any sort of mental calculation. Refreshing your memory shouldn't be too difficult – there are hundreds of maths text books available, and an even large number of excellent maths websites to visit.

Basic maths skills are all very well, but in higher level tests your ability to *reason* with numbers is also being tested. Here are some ways to improve your numerical reasoning ability:

♦ Practise maths with and without a calculator. Practising really does make a difference.

♦ Do number puzzles in newspapers and magazines.

♦ Keep score when playing games like darts, card games etc.

♦ Calculate how much your shopping will cost before you reach the till.

♦ Work out how much change you should receive when you pay for something.

♦ Read financial reports in newspapers.

♦ Study tables of data.

While taking the tests themselves:

♦ Always read the questions themselves very carefully to ensure you understand exactly what it is you are being asked – don't make any assumptions.

♦ Look at the answer choices and quickly eliminate any you know to be incorrect. Concentrate your energies on deciding between the most likely possibilities.

♦ Estimating the solution in your head *before* you look at the answer choices can save you a lot of time and give you confidence that you've chosen correctly.

♦ Numerical reasoning tests demand a high level of concentration and brain work, so treat yourself to a break every now and then. Sit up straight, shut your eyes and take a few deep breaths, just for 20 seconds or so. This will calm you down, relax your back and give your eyes and brain a well deserved rest.

♦ If you really feel that the correct solution is *not* included in the answer choices, take an educated guess and move on. Mistakes on numerical reasoning exam papers do crop up every now and then – psychologists are only human after all!

CHAPTER SIX

Abstract and Non-verbal Reasoning

Abstract reasoning tests, or diagrammatic reasoning tests as they are sometimes called, are psychometric tests which use diagrams, symbols, signs or shapes instead of words and numbers. In other words, they are *visual* questions. And because they require good visual-thinking and logic skills rather than verbal or numerical skills, they are often considered to be a very good indicator of a person's general intellectual ability. For this reason they are given to applicants over a very wide range of jobs, including management.

Abstract reasoning tests measure:

◆ logical analysis
◆ visual thinking
◆ the ability to work through complex problems systematically.

Because they do not require the usual language skills to decode and solve them, they can be used to test more or less anyone, anywhere in the world.

When you look at abstract reasoning tests for the first time, they often appear absolutely impossible to figure out, but on closer inspection you'll see they are not that difficult. To solve sequence questions, for example, you just have to look for patterns. Instead of seeing each illustration as a mass of shapes and symbols, try to work out what each separate element inside the illustration is doing as it progresses through the sequence. Once you 'get' the pattern, you'll be able to work out each specific symbol's next move and look for it in the answer choices.

If all else fails, try figuring out how the questions work with the answers in front of you until you get the idea.

If you really can't see how they work, don't worry. Your chances of landing a management position rest far more on your performance in verbal and numerical reasoning tests, interviews and management exercises. Abstract reasoning tests are a sort of 'added extra' – used by many organisations, but certainly not universally.

Having said that, there are certain types of abstract reasoning questions which are popular with the IT industry. Depending on the job specification, candidates for senior positions are often expected to possess a high level of symbolic reasoning ability together with the capacity to work through complex problems in a systematic and analytical manner. I have included several tests particularly relevant to the IT industry in this chapter.

All abstract reasoning tests are strictly timed, and *every single question will have one, and only one, correct answer.*

In this chapter

In this chapter there are 5 different abstract reasoning tests for you to try. Some are harder than others, and that's an understatement! As mentioned above, several are particularly applicable to the IT industry, and all of them require high-level analytical thinking skills.

At the very end of this chapter there is section entitled **Abstract reasoning tests – how to improve your performance** which is intended to help you do just that across the whole range of abstract reasoning tests. Included in this section are some hints on tackling the questions themselves. If you have a problem with any of the questions then hopefully the advice contained in this section will get you back on track. Remember however that all of us have strengths and weaknesses, and everyone will have some difficulty with some of the tests in this book.

Test 21 Diagrammatic Series

The following test measures your ability to recognise logical sequences within a series of diagrams or symbols.

This type of test is often used to assess reasoning skills at administrative, supervisory and junior management levels – in fact any occupation where logical or analytical reasoning is required. It could be used to select applicants for administrative and supervisory jobs, junior managers, management trainees, and jobs involving technical research or computer programming.

Instructions: Each problem in the test consists of a series of diagrams, on the left of the page, which follow a logical sequence. You are required to choose the next diagram in the series from the five options on the right. Indicate your answer by filling in completely the appropriate circle on the answer sheet.

Time guideline: See how many questions you can answer in 5 minutes. Remember to work accurately as well as quickly.

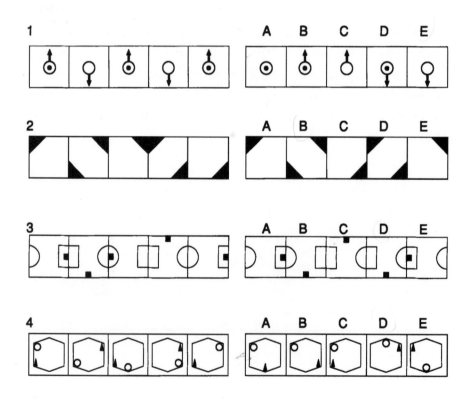

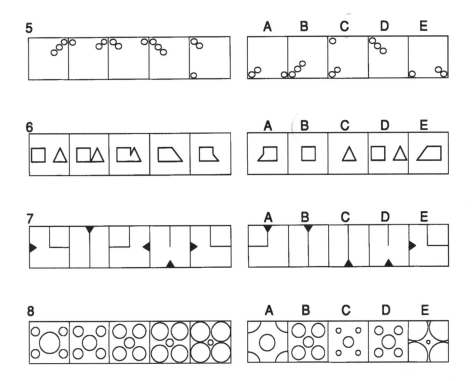

Test 21 Answer Sheet

	A	B	C	D	E
1	Ⓐ	Ⓑ	Ⓒ	Ⓓ	Ⓔ
2	Ⓐ	Ⓑ	Ⓒ	Ⓓ	Ⓔ
3	Ⓐ	Ⓑ	Ⓒ	Ⓓ	Ⓔ
4	Ⓐ	Ⓑ	Ⓒ	Ⓓ	Ⓔ
5	Ⓐ	Ⓑ	Ⓒ	Ⓓ	Ⓔ
6	Ⓐ	Ⓑ	Ⓒ	Ⓓ	Ⓔ
7	Ⓐ	Ⓑ	Ⓒ	Ⓓ	Ⓔ
8	Ⓐ	Ⓑ	Ⓒ	Ⓓ	Ⓔ

Test 22 Diagrammatic Reasoning

This abstract reasoning test measures your ability to infer a set of rules from a flow-chart, and apply these rules to new situations. It is specifically designed for the selection, development and promotion of fairly senior staff working in the IT industry. It is a high-level measure of symbolic reasoning ability and is relevant in jobs that require the capacity to work through complex problems in a systematic and analytical manner, for example, in systems analysis and programming design.

Instructions: In this test you are shown a number of diagrams in which figures (shapes) in BOXES are altered by rules shown as symbols in CIRCLES. The rules can alter each figure by changing its colour, its size, its shape or by turning it upside down.

Paths through each diagram are shown as black or white arrows. You must follow paths which include only one type of arrow.

Work out what each rule does and then answer the questions below each diagram by filling in completely the appropriate circle on the answer sheet.

Time guideline: See how many questions you can answer in 4 minutes.

Look at the example below:

DIAGRAM

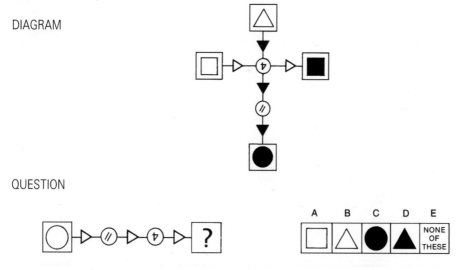

QUESTION

In the diagram, working horizontally, the white square becomes a black square so ⴡ must be a colour changing rule. Working vertically, the white triangle becomes a black circle. Since we know that ⴡ changes the colour of a figure, // must be a shape-changing rule. Applying these rules to the question, it is possible to identify that the white circle becomes a black triangle, so D is the correct answer to the question.

DIAGRAM

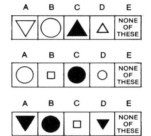

1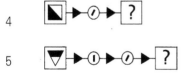

2

3

DIAGRAM

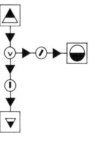

4

5

6

Test 22 Answer Sheet

	A	B	C	D	E			A	B	C	D	E
1	Ⓐ	Ⓑ	Ⓒ	Ⓓ	Ⓔ		4	Ⓐ	Ⓑ	Ⓒ	Ⓓ	Ⓔ
2	Ⓐ	Ⓑ	Ⓒ	Ⓓ	Ⓔ		5	Ⓐ	Ⓑ	Ⓒ	Ⓓ	Ⓔ
3	Ⓐ	Ⓑ	Ⓒ	Ⓓ	Ⓔ		6	Ⓐ	Ⓑ	Ⓒ	Ⓓ	Ⓔ

Test 23 Diagrammatics

Here is another high-level test intended for senior staff being recruited into the IT industry and concerns your ability to reason with diagrams. There is no official time guideline for this test. However work as quickly and as accurately as you can.

Instructions: In this test, figures with BOXES are presented in COLUMNS and are changed in some ways by various commands contained in circles or diamonds. A complete list of these commands and what they do is given in the Command Box below.

Each problem consists of one or more figures in a column. Work down the column, starting at the TOP and dealing with each command and adjacent figure in turn. You must then choose from the five possible answers labelled A to E, the column that results from carrying out the given commands.

There are 10 different command symbols and the effect of each is described and illustrated with an example.

- ◆ Command 1 inverts the figure.
- ◆ Command 2 reverses the figure.
- ◆ Command 3 instructs you to omit the previous figure.
- ◆ Command 4 instructs you to omit the next figure.
- ◆ Command 5 exchanges the contents of the box with the contents of the previous box.
- ◆ Command 6 cancels the previous command.
- ◆ Command 7 cancels the next command.
- ◆ Commands 8, 9 and 10 are contained in **diamonds** and relate to the order on which the complete column of figures is presented.

Command box

Command	Operation
↓	Invert figure
←	Reverse figure
⊕	Omit the previous figure
⊖	Omit the next figure
◯	Swap with previous figure
◆	Cancel the previous command
⊠	Cancel the next command

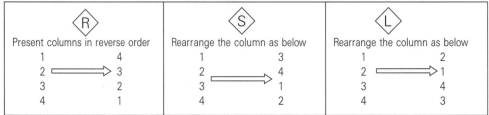

⟨R⟩ Present columns in reverse order	⟨S⟩ Rearrange the column as below	⟨L⟩ Rearrange the column as below
1 → 4	1 → 3	1 → 2
2 → 3	2 → 4	2 → 1
3 → 2	3 → 1	3 → 4
4 → 1	4 → 2	4 → 3

1

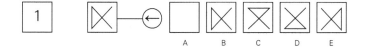

2

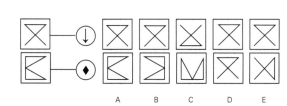

3

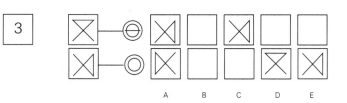

4

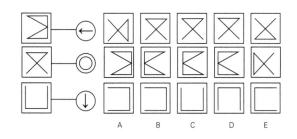

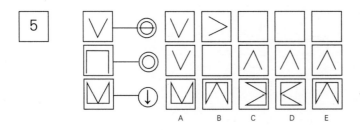

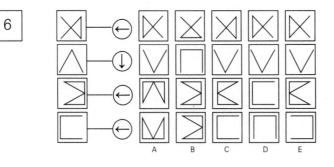

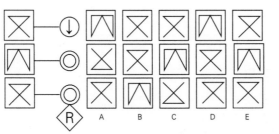

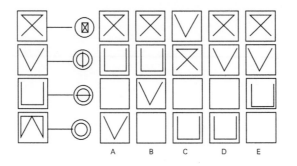

9

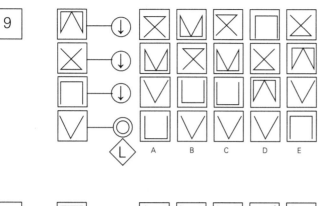

10

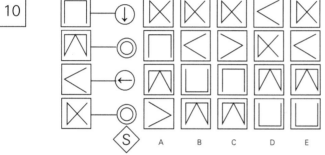

Test 23 Answer Sheet

	A	B	C	D	E
1	Ⓐ	Ⓑ	Ⓒ	Ⓓ	Ⓔ
2	Ⓐ	Ⓑ	Ⓒ	Ⓓ	Ⓔ
3	Ⓐ	Ⓑ	Ⓒ	Ⓓ	Ⓔ
4	Ⓐ	Ⓑ	Ⓒ	Ⓓ	Ⓔ
5	Ⓐ	Ⓑ	Ⓒ	Ⓓ	Ⓔ
6	Ⓐ	Ⓑ	Ⓒ	Ⓓ	Ⓔ
7	Ⓐ	Ⓑ	Ⓒ	Ⓓ	Ⓔ
8	Ⓐ	Ⓑ	Ⓒ	Ⓓ	Ⓔ
9	Ⓐ	Ⓑ	Ⓒ	Ⓓ	Ⓔ
10	Ⓐ	Ⓑ	Ⓒ	Ⓓ	Ⓔ

Test 24 Diagrammatic Reasoning

This test, which is also quite difficult, measures logical and analytical reasoning and requires the recognition of logical rules governing sequences. It is used in the selection of candidates for positions in administration and junior management, for example, office supervisors, senior personal assistants, management trainees, sales and customer service staff, technical research and computer programming. Look at the tips at the end of the chapter if you get stuck.

Instructions: This is a test of reasoning with diagrams. Each problem consists of a series of five diagrams that follow a logical sequence. Your task is to work out which diagram comes next in the series from the five options labelled A–E. Fill in completely the appropriate circle on the answer sheet.

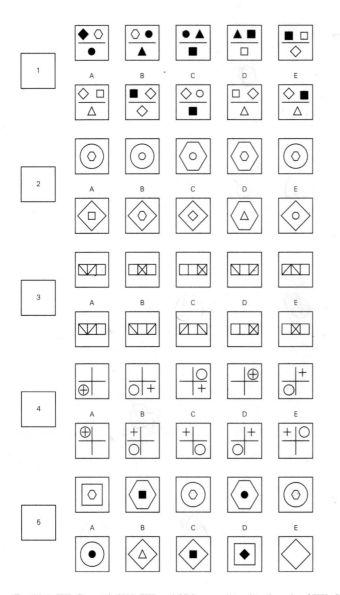

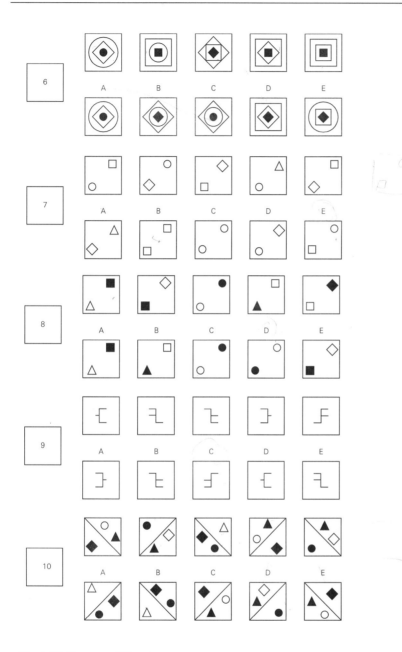

Test 24 Answer Sheet

	A	B	C	D	E			A	B	C	D	E
1	Ⓐ	Ⓑ	Ⓒ	Ⓓ	Ⓔ		6	Ⓐ	Ⓑ	Ⓒ	Ⓓ	Ⓔ
2	Ⓐ	Ⓑ	Ⓒ	Ⓓ	Ⓔ		7	Ⓐ	Ⓑ	Ⓒ	Ⓓ	Ⓔ
3	Ⓐ	Ⓑ	Ⓒ	Ⓓ	Ⓔ		8	Ⓐ	Ⓑ	Ⓒ	Ⓓ	Ⓔ
4	Ⓐ	Ⓑ	Ⓒ	Ⓓ	Ⓔ		9	Ⓐ	Ⓑ	Ⓒ	Ⓓ	Ⓔ
5	Ⓐ	Ⓑ	Ⓒ	Ⓓ	Ⓔ		10	Ⓐ	Ⓑ	Ⓒ	Ⓓ	Ⓔ

Test 25 Diagrammatics

Here is yet another test intended for senior staff being recruited into the IT industry which concerns your ability to reason with diagrams. You will be asked to infer a set of rules from a flow chart and to apply these rules to new situations – a skill which requires a high level of symbolic reasoning ability. It is especially relevant in jobs that require the capacity to work through complex problems in a systematic and analytical manner, for example, in systems analysis and programme design.

Time guideline: There is no official time guideline for this test. However work as quickly and as accurately as you can.

Instructions: This is a test of your ability to infer logically from a symbolic system. In this test there are a number of diagrams. Within each diagram, series of letters are altered in some way by various commands. These commands are represented by symbols. Your task is to work through a diagram; following paths, which are indicated by sets of arrows, in order to determine the effect of the commands and then to answer the questions which follow each diagram. In the test, two different types of arrow are used. When tracing a path between two letter series, you must follow a path that includes only *one* type of arrow.

Please note that each symbol in a diagram has a different meaning. If the same symbol occurs more than once in a diagram, it has the same meaning each time. The meanings of the symbols may differ from one diagram to the next.

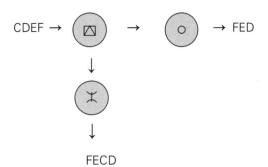

		A	B	C	D	E
1	HIJK → ⊠ → ?	IJK	HJIK	IHJK	KJIH	HJKI
2	MNOP → ⊥ → ?	NOP	NMOP	NOPM	MNOP	MNPO
3	QRST → ○ → ⊥ → ?	QTRS	TQR	QSR	SRQT	TQRS
4	UVWX → ○ → ? → WVU	⊥	⊠	○	⊥ → ⊠	none of these

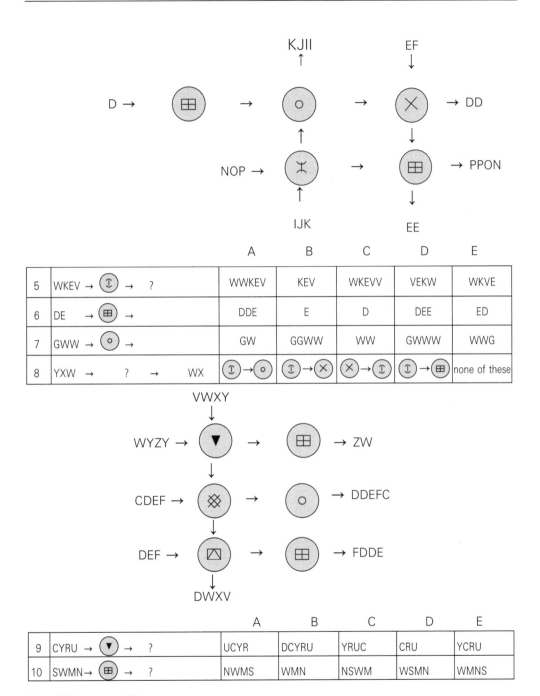

		A	B	C	D	E
5	WKEV → ↻ → ?	WWKEV	KEV	WKEVV	VEKW	WKVE
6	DE → ⊞ →	DDE	E	D	DEE	ED
7	GWW → ⊙ →	GW	GGWW	WW	GWWW	WWG
8	YXW → ? → WX	↻→⊙	↻→✕	✕→↻	↻→⊞	none of these

		A	B	C	D	E
9	CYRU → ▼ → ?	UCYR	DCYRU	YRUC	CRU	YCRU
10	SWMN → ⊞ → ?	NWMS	WMN	NSWM	WSMN	WMNS

Test 25 Answer Sheet

	A	B	C	D	E			A	B	C	D	E
1	Ⓐ	Ⓑ	Ⓒ	Ⓓ	Ⓔ		6	Ⓐ	Ⓑ	Ⓒ	Ⓓ	Ⓔ
2	Ⓐ	Ⓑ	Ⓒ	Ⓓ	Ⓔ		7	Ⓐ	Ⓑ	Ⓒ	Ⓓ	Ⓔ
3	Ⓐ	Ⓑ	Ⓒ	Ⓓ	Ⓔ		8	Ⓐ	Ⓑ	Ⓒ	Ⓓ	Ⓔ
4	Ⓐ	Ⓑ	Ⓒ	Ⓓ	Ⓔ		9	Ⓐ	Ⓑ	Ⓒ	Ⓓ	Ⓔ
5	Ⓐ	Ⓑ	Ⓒ	Ⓓ	Ⓔ		10	Ⓐ	Ⓑ	Ⓒ	Ⓓ	Ⓔ

Answers to abstract reasoning questions

Test 21 Diagrammatic Series

	A	B	C	D	E
1	A	B	C	D	●
2	A	●	C	D	E
3	A	B	C	●	E
4	A	B	C	●	E
5	A	B	●	D	E
6	A	●	C	D	E
7	A	●	C	D	E
8	A	B	C	D	●

Test 22 Diagrammatic Reasoning

	A	B	C	D	E
1	A	●	C	D	E
2	A	B	●	D	E
3	A	B	C	●	E
4	●	B	C	D	E
5	A	B	C	●	E
6	A	B	C	D	●

Test 23 Diagrammatics

	A	B	C	D	E
1	A	B	C	D	●
2	●	B	C	D	E
3	A	B	C	●	E
4	A	B	C	●	E
5	A	B	C	D	●
6	A	B	C	D	●
7	A	●	C	D	E
8	A	B	C	●	E
9	A	B	●	D	E
10	A	B	C	D	●

Test 24 Diagrammatic Reasoning

	A	B	C	D	E
1	A	B	C	●	E
2	A	B	C	D	●
3	A	B	●	D	E
4	A	●	C	D	E
5	●	B	C	D	E
6	A	B	C	D	●
7	A	B	C	D	●
8	A	B	C	●	E
9	A	B	●	D	E
10	●	B	C	D	E

Test 25 Diagrammatics

	A	B	C	D	E
1	A	B	C	●	E
2	A	B	C	D	●
3	A	B	●	D	E
4	A	●	C	D	E
5	A	B	C	●	E
6	●	B	C	D	E
7	A	B	C	●	E
8	A	●	C	D	E
9	A	B	C	●	E
10	A	B	●	D	E

Abstract reasoning tests – how to improve your performance

◆ Try tackling the sort of puzzles in newspapers, magazines and quiz books which involve diagrams.

◆ Play games which involve thinking out a problem visually and in a logical sequence, for example chess, Labyrinth, Tantrix, or computer Freecell.

◆ Abstract reasoning questions are often presented as sequences. Some are straightforward, but others require you to regard each shape, line, or symbol as a separate component working in its own independent way. For example you might have a circle moving in a clockwise direction, and a triangle going anticlockwise. Or one shape moving two spaces each time, another moving one space at a time.

◆ Watch out for shapes or lines which move first in one direction, then another direction. Or shapes which alternate between hollow and filled in, or appear on the outside of an illustration, then the inside etc.

◆ Don't be fazed by weird looking symbols or shapes, just study them until you see the pattern and how it changes from one illustration to the next. If you can work out what each separate element inside the illustration is doing as it progresses through the sequence, you can then predict how that component will appear in the next illustration in the series.

◆ People with dyslexia are often very good at abstract reasoning. They may have some difficulty with words, but when it comes to logic, they're better than anyone else.

If you work, or want to work, in IT you will need the key tools of the trade – programming languages, technologies and operating environments – so perhaps learn some of the following:

◆ Programming languages such as HTML, XML / XSL, Basic, Visual Basic, C++, Java, .NET (including : ASP.NET, C# (pronounced 'Cee sharp'), VB.NET) and use them as much as possible.

♦ Relational database skills such as SQL, T-SQL.

Here's an additional list of languages and technologies to consider:

♦ Scripting: Javascript, VBScript, Perl.
♦ Web: HTTP, HTML, XML, XSL, ASP, JSP, Servlets, J2EE, .NET.
♦ Interactive web and CD-ROM: Macromedia Flash and Director.
♦ Web services: WSDL, SOAP.
♦ Componentware: DCOM, COM+, EJB.
♦ Databases: SQL Server, Oracle, DB2, Sybase.
♦ EAI: Oracle, SAP, Ariba, Agresso, CedAr.
♦ Mail systems: Exchange, Domino, ESMTP, X.400.
♦ Directory systems: LDAP, X.500, Active Directory.
♦ Security infrastructure: PKI, SSL, Kerberos, PGP.
♦ Windows platforms: 95, 98, NT, 2000, XP.
♦ Unix platforms: Solaris, Linux, AIX, HP-UX, Mac OS X.

For all these ideas there's simply no substitute for hands-on practical experience. Skill in this area is all about the application of logical deduction, coupled with common sense, patience and curiosity. If you already possess those qualities, **practical experience** – i.e. using the programmes or languages as much as possible – is the thing which will most improve your performance in this area.

PART TWO
Management Tests and Exercises – Your Visit to the Assessment Centre

Assessment Events and Assessment Centres

This must sound like a very confused chapter title – however assessment 'events' and assessment 'centres' are totally different things.

Assessment events

An assessment event, or an assessment day, is HR (Human Resources/Personnel) jargon for getting a large number of candidates together at the employer's premises, or more usually an outside location such as a hotel, in order for them to take a variety of psychometric tests, en masse. Candidates may also be required to complete a personality questionnaire and subjected to one or two short interviews (which could include feedback and discussion about your test results) but that's basically it.

The assessment event usually takes *less* than a day – perhaps a couple of hours or so.

Assessment events are generally used to test large numbers of candidates (50 or more) and whittle the numbers down to manageable levels. Having said that, it's unlikely that you will be invited along to an assessment event until you have already passed the initial screening process, which will probably have included you submitting your CV and perhaps taking a number of ability-type psychometric and personality tests online. The assessment event is the next stage in the recruitment process.

A good example of where assessment events are used pretty frequently is in the selection of candidates for graduate programmes and other fast-track junior management schemes. HR people sometimes call it the 'multiple hurdle' approach – another example of industry jargon.

Once you've completed the tests and interviews, you'll go home and wait to be contacted by the organisation. Usually they'll let you know very quickly whether they would like to progress your application any further or not.

You might be wondering why all this testing couldn't be done online, or why you have to be re-tested at an assessment event when you've *already* taken, and passed, the online tests. Why should you have to take time off to attend an assessment event with all the hassle of preparing and travelling there and back?

The answer to this is simple – it's all a matter of control. Whereas online tests are simple to administer and relatively cheap, the downside is the possibility that you could have cheated. How do they know it was you who took the online test and not your best friend who just happens to be, say, a maths wizard? Even employers who use online testing extensively are paranoid about this. Getting you physically into an exam room is the only way they can really reassure themselves that you are who you say you are, and that your performance is genuine.

For this reason online testing is certainly becoming more and more popular with employers, but the assessment event isn't likely to go away any day soon.

Assessment centres

Assessment centre, however, is HR jargon for getting a *much smaller* group of *short-listed* candidates together – again, either at the employer's premises, or an outside location such as a hotel – and subjecting them to an intensive battery of tests and exercises as a more advanced part of the recruitment process. The purpose is to assess your managerial skills and style, and also to identify areas of particular strength (or relative weakness).

The assessment centre visit usually takes the best part of a whole day, but quite often candidates are asked to stay overnight and sit more tests the following day. Talk about tough...

The good news is that once you've got to this stage in the process you can feel fairly confident that the organisation in question is seriously interested in you.

Note: Sometimes the term 'development centre' is used instead. In fact, many HR people refer to the assessment centre as a process, not a place.

What happens at the assessment centre?

You can expect a number of things to happen, not necessarily in this order:

1   You may have to take a number of **ability-type psychometric tests**. These will be taken in exam-like conditions and be strictly timed. Some of these tests could be the same, or very similar to those you have already taken online, others will be longer and more difficult.

     For managerial positions you will normally be expected to take exams in verbal reasoning, numerical reasoning, and possibly abstract reasoning. Practice material for these is covered from **Chapter Four** onwards.

2   You will also be expected to complete at least one **personality questionnaire** (see **Chapter Eleven**).

3   Assuming you are applying for a managerial position, you will take one or more **management test**. Tests such as in-tray exercises and scenario-type tests, you will take individually, probably in an exam room (although it's possible you'll have somebody from the recruiting organisation with you, discussing the test as you go along).

     Other tests, such as presentations, will require you to 'perform' in front of assessors and possibly other candidates as well. Furthermore, you're virtually guaranteed to be involved in one or more group exercise in which all candidates work together as a team. While you all work and interact, the selectors will observe everyone's performance.

     Management tests and exercises are covered in **Chapters Nine and Ten**.

4   Next, you can expect to be **interviewed**. Interviews may also include feedback and discussion about your test results or performance in the group exercises. You may be interviewed by one person, a panel, or both. Assessment *centre* interviews are usually longer and much more intense than the ones you will experience at an assessment *event*. Interviews are also discussed briefly in **Chapter Ten**.

5   Because the assessment centre takes place over the course of several hours, even days, you can expect to participate in various **social events**. By this I mean time spent in the company of the assessors and the other candidates – relaxing, eating, perhaps playing sport, having a drink in the evening, taking part in informal discussions etc. The social aspect of the assessment centre is just as important as the testing and is discussed later on in this chapter.

Obviously the number, type and difficulty of the tests and exercises will depend very much upon the level of seniority and areas of responsibility that the job you're applying for involves.

How likely is it that I will have to go through the assessment centre process?

Assessment centres are used to assess short-listed candidates (and graduates) into junior, middle and senior management positions.

In fact, the more senior the job you are applying for, the more likely it is that you will be required to attend an assessment centre appointment, and the longer and more rigorous your assessment will be.

Will I be told what to expect in advance?

Yes. Candidates are normally given detailed information about assessment centre appointments in advance. As well as receiving a general agenda, you should also be told what sort of tests to expect and whether or not you need to prepare a specific presentation.

If the information is not forthcoming, ring up and ask. Obviously details like addresses, timings, where to park etc. should be given to you as a matter of course.

Why do employers like assessment centres so much?

Employers worldwide view the assessment centre as an excellent predictor of job performance. Not only can they rigorously test the most promising candidates in all sorts of ways, they also have the luxury of observing their behaviour and social skills over a fairly long period of time. You, and other candidates will be working under exam-like conditions, taking part in group exercises, relaxing, eating, and often completely off-guard.

More than anything else, the recruiter has an opportunity to interact with and get to know each candidate reasonably well – something that simply cannot be done during the course of an interview.

Obviously, from an employer's point of view this is a very good thing indeed; they can feel confident that at the end of the process they'll end up with the perfect person for the job.

What does an assessor do?

Assessors (or selectors) are people who run the assessment centre. Apart from ensuring the whole thing runs smoothly, they also sit on the sidelines and assess your performance in every type of management test, group exercises or presentation. They are also responsible for interviewing candidates, or talking them through individual management exercises.

The assessors are normally people from the recruiting organisation, however there could be one or two who've been brought in to actually run the assessment centre. They are normally highly trained and intelligent, and also very personable – after all part of their job is to make you and other candidates feel relaxed and comfortable.

How many assessors will be there?

Ideally an assessment centre is one where there is a 2:1 ratio of candidates to assessors, and no one assessor observes the same candidate twice.

And how many candidates?

There could be up to eight other candidates being assessed with you. Sometimes organisations invite a larger number and then split them up into separate groups for the actual tests.

Will I get to meet my new boss?

You might – it all depends on the job. If you're going for a specific managerial position, then yes, you're quite likely to meet and be interviewed by your new boss. If you're one of a batch of graduates being recruited onto a graduate or junior management programme, then no, it's unlikely.

What's in it for me?

As far as you are concerned, the assessment centre also has some very big advantages. You get a chance to demonstrate your key skills in a variety of areas, something that would be impossible to do during an interview on its own. You get to meet lots of people from your target organisation. You get a chance to be assessed fairly and without bias.

You also get the chance to assess *them*. By the end of your visit you should have a pretty clear idea about whether you still want to work for them or not.

You will be in a position to ask for feedback on the psychometric and personality tests you've just taken, which will give you a clearer idea of how an employer views your strengths and weaknesses. You'll also be able to discuss your performance in the management tests and exercises.

Even if you're not offered a job you should definitely benefit from the experience, even if it's just the added confidence of knowing what to expect next time.

What about very senior management positions?

The recruitment process into the most senior levels of management often bypasses some of the earlier stages of the normal recruitment process, such as the online testing and assessment event sifting. At director-level, people are often headhunted or come via specialist recruitment agencies. If this sounds like you, you should still expect to encounter some testing, especially role plays and individual management scenario-type tests. You might escape the group tests and exercises, but you'll definitely be subjected to intense scrutiny during individual testing and one-on-one interviews.

Preparing for your visit

Whether you are going to an assessment event or a full-blown assessment centre appointment, the following tips will help you get the most out of the experience. Actual tests and exercises are covered from **Chapter Nine** onwards.

Be prepared

As mentioned above, most companies automatically tell you exactly what to expect during your assessment centre visit – in fact it's regarded as good practice to do so. However, if no information is forthcoming, you'll need to take the initiative. Simply call up their HR department (or your prospective new boss) and ask for more information. Ask about the tests and exercises you'll be taking, and whether they can send you any sample material. It's as simple as that.

If you get the opportunity, ask about the job, and the organisation as well. Personnel managers are usually, by the very nature of their jobs, friendly and approachable, and it's extremely unlikely that they'll object to helping you. So long as you are polite and entirely professional, there is no reason why you shouldn't be successful every time.

Not only have you nothing to lose, phoning up could give you a clear advantage in more ways than one. If you know what to expect you'll be better prepared, not to mention more relaxed. From the employer's point of view you will have become a candidate who is showing interest and is serious about the job – exactly the sort of person they want.

One very useful thing you can do in advance is to **research** the organisation in question. This is quite a large topic, so I've allocated it the next chapter all to itself. However thoroughly you research you're bound to still have some unanswered questions, so note them down and take them with you.

Plan your journey/route

Make sure you've got the exact address, and good directions. And find out which bus or train to take, or where to park if you're driving. Always allow extra time for tractors, jack-knifed lorries and those awful temporary traffic lights which seem to materialise overnight. The same applies to bus and rail journeys. Trust me, if a train is going to cancelled, it'll be yours.

Perhaps if you have the time and it's not too far away, it might be an idea to visit the location of the assessment centre a few days before to get your 'bearings'.

Get organised

Decide what you're going to wear *before* the day in question, shine your shoes, sort out your briefcase, find your glasses, and if you're going to be staying overnight, pack your overnight bag...very carefully. The last thing you'll want is to discover you've forgotten your toothbrush.

Also take a decent pen, a calculator, and perhaps a copy of the CV you sent the organisation in question (to remind yourself of what you told them!).

If you have any sort of disability you might also consider telling the selectors before the day, so that they can make arrangements in advance. For example, if you use a wheelchair, most organisations will arrange for your testing to take place on the ground floor – but you have to tell them beforehand. The same goes for dyslexia, special diets etc.

Relax

Laughter is a great cure for nervous tension, so perhaps rent an amusing DVD or go to see a film the night before. But do try to get a reasonable night's sleep. Alternatively, get some exercise and follow it up with a long soak in the bath.

On the day itself

Have a good breakfast

Include simple sugars (fruit juice) and complex carbohydrates (toast or cereal) and possibly some protein (milk, eggs, cheese or meat). This will keep your blood sugar stable and your energy levels up. I know it can be difficult to think about food when you're nervous but do try to eat *something*.

Later on, if you're staying for a whole day or more, you'll be provided with refreshments. Again, try to eat sensibly and have plenty to drink (obviously I don't mean alcohol). Studies have proved that water helps your mind stay alert – that's why many schools insist on kids carrying around bottles of water all day long. Tea also works.

Look smart

One of the best ways to boost your self-confidence is to look smart. Remember you are a manager, so aim to look the part: well turned-out, professional and confident...and no jeans! A briefcase is infinitely preferable to a scruffy plastic bag to carry around your bits and pieces.

Even if you're absolutely certain that you're not going to be interviewed or asked to give a presentation, it's still important to make an effort with your appearance. You'll feel better for it too.

If you're really unsure about what to wear, you can always ring the HR department and ask for a few tips on dress code. But generally, at least in the UK, most business managers (men and women) wear suits.

Be punctual

Arrive on time. Both assessment events and assessment centres are generally run to very tight deadlines, and you will usually find that the centre kicks off with tests which you simply cannot start a few minutes after everyone else.

Also consider the impression your lateness will make on your prospective employer. It's most unlikely they will fall over themselves to recruit somebody who's incapable of turning up on time – what sort of example will that set to junior staff?

Of course if something does genuinely delay you, be professional and ring the organisation, apologise, explain and give your approximate arrival time.

The social aspect of the assessment centre – being friendly

Taking tests, being interviewed, giving presentations and problem-solving alongside other applicants is very stressful, but be assured everyone else will be feeling as nervous as you. Even the assessors will be a little strained – it's actually quite a demanding job.

So make it easier for yourself by being sociable, friendly and likeable. Chatting to the other candidates and the people from the recruiting company will not only help to overcome your nerves, it will help your chances of landing the job too. Asking intelligent questions, appearing interested in the organisation, being generally good company – all these things are just as important as passing the tests.

The fact that you have a chance to talk to existing staff gives you a great opportunity to find out all sorts of things about the organisation, its policies, ethos and culture, although you will have some of this information already if you've done your homework properly (see the next chapter – **Researching Your Chosen Organisation** for more information).

You can also use the opportunity to chat to other candidates, thereby developing your effective networking skills. You never know when you might meet up with them again on another occasion.

Dos and don'ts

This must sound obvious, but you'd be surprised how many candidates let themselves down by behaving badly. If you're staying at a hotel overnight, try not to drink the bar dry. Nobody will hire you if you turn up the next morning with a hangover.

Other *don'ts* include overeating, telling sexist or racist jokes, swearing, criticising your current boss, smoking unless invited to, or seducing one of the assessors (wait until you've got the job!).

Always respect other people. This means being friendly towards everyone you meet, not just the assessors. Sometimes candidates (amazingly) try to intimidate other candidates by hogging the conversation or steamrollering over anything that they say. This will not endear you to anyone. Also respect the staff at the venue – basically treat everyone as you'd like to be treated yourself.

Lastly, if you want to be on top form in the morning – don't go to bed too late.

What if I'm a shy person?

What if, rather than socialising and chatting to people you've never met before, you'd rather curl up by the fire and read a book?

As mentioned above, an assessment centre is a good opportunity to meet people already working for the organisation so it would be a shame to miss out on the chance to socialise and get to know them. Chatting to other candidates is also worthwhile. It may seem hugely difficult to walk over to somebody, say 'hi' and start a conversation, but you're quite likely to discover that the other person is a) pleasant, b) interesting, c) feeling just as inadequate/apprehensive/nervous as you are.

Also, remind yourself that as a manager, you will doubtless be expected to talk to people and get on with them on a daily basis. This does *not* mean that all managers are required to be loud, extrovert types, but it would be true to say that good managers are usually good communicators.

As far as staying very quiet in the actual group exercises is concerned, there you might have a bit of a problem. The selectors will find it very difficult to evaluate you and your ability to manage if you contribute absolutely nothing to the proceedings. Rather than envying all those talkative types and feeling inadequate, be brave and remember that a small number of well thought-out, pertinent, useful comments are actually preferable to a torrent of meaningless drivel which some people employ to mask the fact that they have no idea what they're talking about.

Staying cool

And what if your knees are still shaking? Here are a few useful relaxation exercises that will help you handle the stress. With a little practice, you'll be able to use them anywhere; in the car, on the bus, in the exam room...

1 **Breathing exercise**
   Breathe in slowly to really fill your lungs. Hold your breath for three seconds, then slowly breathe out through your mouth. As you breathe out, imagine all the tension and stress flowing out with the air. Repeat two or three times.

2 **Tension release exercise**
   Tense the muscle groups one by one, and then relax them. Begin with your feet: screw up your toes as tightly as possible and hold for three or four seconds. Then slowly relax. Continue upwards through your body, working your legs, your stomach, your hands, your arms, your shoulders and even your face.

3 **Tension release exercise number 2**
   This is a good last-minute exercise to use while you're waiting to be called into the test room, or just before you give a presentation. Simply go to the toilet, make sure no one can see you (trust me you do *not* want an audience for this) and make yourself shake like a jelly. I mean really, physically shake your whole body for at least 20 seconds. Pretend you're auditioning for a low-budget horror movie. Then stop, take a few slow, deep breaths, and off you go. I guarantee you'll suddenly feel incredibly calm and composed and ready for anything.

What will happen after the assessment event or assessment centre?

After the whole thing is over you can go home and relax. Actually you'll need to – assessment centres can be extremely challenging and you're bound to feel thoroughly worn out. The assessors however, usually have to stay on for some time, discussing and evaluating each candidate in terms of their performance in the tests and exercises they've participated in. This is often referred to as a *wash-up* session.

Usually the recruiting organisation will let you know very quickly whether they would like to progress your application any further or not.

How do I get feedback?

If you are attending an assessment centre as part of ongoing job development you should receive detailed information about your performance in the tests and exercises. If you have attended as part of a selection procedure you should be offered feedback, regardless of whether or not you are successful. However, not all organisations have a policy of freely offering feedback to candidates – it may not be forthcoming unless you actually ask. Check with the test administrator at the assessment centre for details.

Don't be surprised if they will not discuss anything with you there and then. This is because with management tests and exercises, it's not just about raw scores or how many questions you got right, it's also all to do with your management style, personality and ability to relate well to other people etc. This cannot be discussed or decided upon until after you, and all the other candidates, have gone home.

But there's nothing to stop you picking up the phone after a few days, if you haven't heard anything.

And if you haven't been successful, please remember that to reach the assessment centre you would have done extremely well, and hopefully gained a lot of very useful experience.

CHAPTER EIGHT

Researching Your Chosen Organisation

What's a sure fire way to inspire confidence in your suitability to manage? To convince your future boss that you are the *one*? How is it possible to find out what qualities and abilities an organisation is looking for in its managers? Or what it's really like to work for them?

Not by reading the job ad, that's for sure.

The only way to discover everything about a job, the people, the culture, the ethos, the aims and the successes (or otherwise) of a company, is by **researching**.

In the previous chapter I discussed ways of preparing for your assessment event or assessment centre visit. Researching is one of the best ways of doing this.

Note: Good research skills are also extremely valuable when it comes to preparing a presentation. These are covered in Chapter Ten.

Why research?

Why bother? Here are some very good reasons:

◆ Managerial qualities include the ability to lead, to take the business forward, to plan for future success. You can't do that unless you are fully conversant with the product or service your target organisation offers, the state of the market and what its competitors are up to. It's no good waiting until you get the job – you won't be taken seriously unless you can demonstrate that you know about these things now.

◆ Managerial qualities also include the ability to think, to find out and analyse information, and to form opinions – and researching is all of these things. If you are unable or unwilling to do it, perhaps management isn't for you.

◆ You can use the information you acquire during your research to enhance your CV and tailor your job application. You'll also be able to put it to good use during interviews and assessment centre visits where you will be able to talk knowledgeably and with conviction.

♦ Researching will enable you to give every organisation you apply to a thoroughly convincing answer to the most important interview question of all; *'Why do you want to work for us?'*

What to research

The main goal of your research should be to discover as much as possible about the following:

♦ Your target organisation's products or services and how they are sold and marketed.
♦ How successful the organisation is and the state of their finances.
♦ How they stand in relation to their competitors/market share.
♦ What's happening in the industry.
♦ What their staff think about them.
♦ What it's really like to work there.

How *much* research you do will obviously depend on the type of job you are applying for, the area in which you will be working, and the level of seniority you're after. For example, an office manager will need a general overview of the firm's product or service, but a finance director will require much more detailed knowledge such as the financial position of the firm, its performance on the stock market and the state of the industry it operates in.

How to research

Here are lots of ideas for getting that vital information fairly quickly and easily:

1. Look at what the company does

If they are a retailer, visit the stores. If they make a product, have a look at it, examine it, use it. If they offer a service, try it out, or talk to people who have. Look at the company's advertising material, read their leaflets, browse through their catalogues (just ring up and ask for one). Get a feel for what they're all about, then decide what you think of it all. What are their good points? What about the not-so-good? How do they compare with their competitors?

For example, say your target organisation is a supermarket chain – what do you like about their operation? Think about their brands, the packaging, the pricing, the layout of stores. Are they tidy, well stocked, clean, peopled by intelligent, helpful staff? Or do the shelves lack basic provisions, are the queues miles long. Some supermarkets can process a fully-loaded shopping trolley in the time it takes others to put through for one miserable item. Customers are fickle – basic, obvious mistakes can quickly change a company's fortunes.

If your target organisation's product is not readily available or visible on the high street, it's still easy enough to find out everything you want to know. Say they manufacture something totally obscure, like pH meters, simply ring up and ask for a catalogue and their web address. Then, with a broadband connection and a few minutes to spare, you should be able to discover everything you always wanted to know about pH meters; not only what they do but what they look like, how much they cost, who sells them, who is the market and so on.

Note: To find any company website, either use a search engine such as www.google.co.uk, or try www.kellysearch.com which lists contact details, descriptions and links to thousands of UK companies. Or simply ring up and ask.

2. Find out how successful they are

It's always a good idea to find out how successful (or not) your chosen company is, no matter what job you're after. Never assume that just because they're a household name, their balance sheet is super healthy and they must be doing OK. It isn't necessarily so.

Financial information is not just for accountants, it's for everyone with an interest in an organisation, especially its potential managers. Discovering that your target company is a highly successful market leader could make you keener to work there (and there's nothing wrong with telling them that either). Uncovering the fact that they're struggling to survive might put you off completely. It would put *me* off.

There are lots of ways of taking a company's financial temperature. First of all, **read the financial press**, for a broad overview of what's happening in the world of money. If you want to access information on your chosen organisation instantly, go to the web. Most newspapers have websites with searchable archives, and some, such as the *Financial Times*, allow you to search newspapers and trade journals from around the world, free of charge. Some UK based newspaper websites are:

www.guardian.co.uk
www.independent.co.uk
www.ft.com
www.thetimes.co.uk

If you're conversant with all things financial and you'd like to dig a little deeper, check out your chosen organisation's accounts. To view a UK limited (ltd) or public limited company (plc) accounts, you'll need to pay a visit to **Companies House**. They have branches around the country or you can call the Companies House Contact Centre on 0870 33 33 636 or email them on enquiries@companies-house.gov.uk but the easiest way is simply to go online at www.companieshouse.gov.uk and order the information you require. For around £5 or so you can download latest filed accounts and other financial information in PDF or TIFF format. Some of the basic stuff is free, and almost 2 million UK companies are registered.

The only downside to the Companies House reports is that they are fairly raw and come without very much explanation – you may be better to find a credit-check firm to provide you with a more user-friendly report. The quickest way to find one is to search on the web for 'credit check companies' and you'll get a huge list. A report containing all you need to know about a business's financial standing, credit worthiness, directors, shareholders and company history is easy to come by, although it won't be cheap.

If your target organisation is a plc it will often be listed on the **Stock Exchange**. This means you can check out its share price and compare it to its competitors'. You don't need a maths degree to spot a company thriving or failing.

Listed companies also produce an **annual report**. This is basically a glossy report on the company's activities over the previous year and should include company accounts, director listings, details of political and charitable donations etc. It should also give you information about the company's major projects, its brands, number of employees etc, all fairly one-sided but useful nevertheless. To get one free of charge, simply ring up the company's head office and request they send you one (ask for the latest annual report and interim report). Some companies post annual reports on their websites.

Companies not listed on the Stock Exchange may still produce an annual report, especially publicly-owned companies.

3. Investigate the industry/market.

This is where you investigate how successful your target organisation is in relation to its competitors. It's also about finding out what's happening in the specific industry – is it on a roll or is it in trouble? Of course, if you work in the same industry you'll already have a lot of the answers, but you may still need them in a lot more detail if you're moving up the corporate ladder. I've already suggested share price comparisons, but you can also do the following:

    Trade associations and professional institutes usually have information services which you can phone up for statistics, market data and other relevant information. They also have websites and magazines/journals which discuss news and major developments in their industry.

    Market research companies. The market research reports most commonly found in UK libraries are those published by Keynote (www.keynote.co.uk). Mintel (www.mintel.co.uk) is another important UK publisher. Both the Keynote and Mintel websites have databases where you can search for relevant titles and executive summaries of the reports.

    Company newsletters are also a great source of up-to-date information. They go out to all employees and cover all sorts of issues relevant to the company, including details of major contracts, industry awards, market news, management issues, new training schemes, office relocations etc and are well worth a phone call to an HR department at the head office to request a copy.

    Another way to get the information is to ring up and ask. **Press Office** staff should know who the competitors are and may be quite happy to talk to you if you explain you're researching before applying for a job. All you need is someone chatty and in the know, with 5 minutes to spare. The worst that can happen is you get somebody uncooperative or ignorant, but generally most people are helpful and friendly.

4. Find out what it's like to work for them

As mentioned above, **company newsletters** are a great source of information and can probably give you a pretty good idea about the corporate culture as well as the latest company news. Staff facilities, perks and awards usually feature highly too.

While you're on the phone requesting a company newsletter, why not be a bit chatty. People working in HR departments are usually extremely friendly and will often be happy to talk to you about the organisation and what it's like to work there.

Many organisations have sections on their **web sites** featuring interviews with current employees, especially graduate recruits and junior managers. They also often feature pages upon pages of company blurb about why it's a great place to work – obviously totally biased, but it will give you some idea about what to expect and help you formulate lots of questions to ask at interview.

Look out for **newspaper supplements** devoted to comparing major companies, their work ethos and culture. The *Sunday Times* regularly publishes supplements such as 'Top Companies', 'Fastest Growing Companies' etc, and so do other newspapers. You can also try searching the web for the various '**employer awards**'.

Obviously if you are offered the chance to 'shadow' an employee, you should jump at the chance. The very best way to find out what it's like to work for a specific employer is to actually get some hands on experience with them.

5. Investigate their recruitment processes

If you're still keen, you'll need to find out as much as you can about the job itself, not to mention the company recruitment procedure. If you think all the information you need is contained in the job ad, think again. It might give you a basic idea, but that's all. If you would like to dig a little deeper, you'll need to get hold of the **job spec and applicant profile** from the company's HR department (or relevant department).

A 'job spec' is a detailed list of all the responsibilities of the actual position, and an 'applicant spec' or 'applicant profile' will describe the qualities and abilities the organisation hopes the successful candidate will possess.

It's not always possible to get hold of this information – but what have you got to lose by ringing up and asking for it? As mentioned above, HR staff are usually very happy to talk to you about the companies they work for, and even if you can't get the 'person spec' you should be able to pick up plenty of other valuable information to help you in your application.

You should also be able to pick up a huge amount of information on their recruitment process by studying their **company web site**, such as the hoops you'll have to jump through in order to get an interview, ie online application, personality and ability tests, perhaps a telephone interview, assessment event, more psychometric tests...sounds daunting, but at least you'll be prepared.

You'll also be able to discover things such as:

- How important industry experience is to them.
- What personal qualities and abilities they are looking for.
- The career development and training on offer.
- Location of their offices, manufacturing plants, etc.
- Whether managers are expected to be flexible when it comes to location, etc.
- Rates of pay, perks, staff facilities and so on.
- Management structure and hierachy.
- What the hours are like...and much, much more.

Finally

Sit back and ask yourself whether it all fits in with your expectations. Do you still like what you see? Are you still as enthusiastic about working for your target organisation as you were before you began your research? Do you now have a clearer idea of how your particular knowledge, experience and management skills could benefit your chosen company? Have you any ideas about the direction you'd like to take them, if you had the chance?

If you value your happiness, these vitally important questions need to be asked and answered. Even if the conclusion you come to is that you'd much rather work for one of their competitors, it's still a very valuable exercise.

CHAPTER NINE

Management Tests

This chapter contains a management test FAQ and also samples of management tests and exercises that you will encounter during your assessment centre appointment. These include examples of SHL's *Brainstorm*, *Fastrack* and *Scenerios* tests – all very well known and extremely popular management tests used by a huge number of organisations to select both graduate recruits and more senior management staff.

Information on how to tackle the questions are included before and after each particular type of test. Please remember however that all of us have strengths and weaknesses, and everyone will have some difficulty with some of the tests in this book.

At the very end of the *next* chapter there is section entitled **Management tests and exercises – how to improve your performance** in which I explain ways in which you can improve your management skills without taking a management or business degree, and yes, it is possible!

Management test FAQ

How do management tests differ from psychometric tests?

Basically, management tests are more hands-on. Instead of filling in, or clicking, multiple choice boxes, you write down your answers in the space provided on the test paper. Sometimes you are required to discuss your answers and rationale to an examiner rather than writing down anything at all. Another difference is that management tests usually require pretty hard thinking and also a certain amount of know-how. Unlike psychometric tests which all come in multiple choice format, there are only limited opportunities to guess the answers.

Are management tests always taken in exam-like conditions?

Yes and no. It all depends upon the organisation. Sometimes you'll find yourself sitting in an exam room all on your own, but you're equally likely to find yourself accompanied by a member of the recruiting organisation. This individual will be there to help and discuss the issues with you throughout the test. This doesn't mean the test is easier; far from it. Discussing the test as you work through it will reveal your thinking processes as well as any problems and dilemmas you have. Remember when you did maths at school and the teachers insisted on you showing your workings? Well this is a sort of grown-up version of the same thing.

For what sort of job would I be expected to take a management test?

The tests and exercises in this chapter are used to assess people applying for managerial jobs, ranging from the graduate seeking a foothold on the management ladder to the more experienced boss looking for a more senior position. Management tests are used across the whole spectrum of different industries around the globe and are especially applicable whenever analytical and problem-solving skills are a requirement of the job. If you want to get into management, this is what you're going to encounter on your journey.

How difficult will the tests be?

As I've mentioned before, the number, type and difficulty of the tests and exercises will depend very much upon the level of seniority and areas of responsibility that the job you're applying for involves. For all jobs, expect to have your general managerial abilities tested as well as specific skills.

What do management tests measure?

Management tests measure:

◆ Whether you know how to manage.

◆ What sort of management style you possess.

◆ How creative you are.

◆ How well you evaluate information.

◆ How logically you are able to make decisions.

◆ How good you are at generating ideas and problem-solving strategies.

◆ How well you work under pressure...get the picture?

Like traditional multiple choice psychometric tests they also provide employers with a good indication of a) whether a candidate has the right skills or aptitude for the job, and b) whether or not they will be successful in the job itself.

Who devises management tests?

They are usually written by the same test publishers who produce the traditional type of psychometric test, such as SHL Group plc. Having said that, many organisations employ a sort of mix and match approach to the testing. They might buy a few off-the-shelf tests and have the rest developed specifically for them, i.e. they might pay a test publisher to customise a particular test to assess the particular skills needed to carry out the job.

They might also use their own material. For example, it's quite normal for an in-tray exercise to be carried out using the actual contents of one of the existing manager's in-trays.

Overall, this means that a management test taken at company A is very unlikely to be identical to a management test taken at company B.

Do management tests have right and wrong answers?

Some of them do, some of them don't. Sometimes the right answer for company A will be the wrong answer for company B. It all depends upon the ethos, culture, management style, company goals and so on, of the organisation in question. See the individual tests and exercises for clarification.

To get a (slightly) clearer picture of what a specific organisation is looking for you are advised to do some research – see **Chapter Eight** for information on how to do this.

What if I completely mess up one of the tests?

Be assured that the assessors expect the testing process to reveal your individual strengths and weaknesses. Luckily you can normally compensate for a bad performance in one area by excelling in another.

If you feel that you've let yourself down, speak to one of the assessors about it. They might ask you about it anyway during an interview. Be honest about the difficulty you had and try to show that you've learned something from the experience. Whatever you do, don't give up and go home.

Where will I encounter a management test?

Generally you will be asked to take this type of test when you are invited by a potential employer to come along to their offices or to attend an **assessment centre**.

In other words, you will not encounter any of these tests until you are well into the recruitment process and have already passed through your target organisation's initial screening process. It is extremely unlikely that you will ever be asked to take one of these tests online.

The *Brainstorm* tests

This is a very popular and widely used 'paper and pencil' management test. It is designed to assess how productive an individual can be when coming up with ideas. In other words, your breadth of thinking. *Brainstorm* is used to assess graduates for junior and slightly more senior management roles, especially those requiring analytical and problem-solving skills.

It consists of a number of work situations, or problems. What you have to do is read each work situation or problem, and then try to generate as many alternative options to the problem as you can in **four** minutes.

Sometimes the question will ask you for solutions to the problem. Other times it will ask you for explanations of factors that need to be investigated further. This will always be stated clearly in the question.

Four minutes per question is not very long (actually it's a deliberate ploy to put you under pressure) so work quickly and try not to dwell too long on each answer.

How are answers assessed?

There are no right or wrong answers as such, provided they are meaningful and relevant. Any organisation which presents you with this type of test will assess you on three things; the number and variety of answers you give, and their originality.

To sum it up, you are being assessed on your breadth and depth of solutions that are relevant. If you can explain your solutions in more detail, then go for it, but don't waste precious time on just two or three answers.

What if some of my answers are completely impractical?

Brainstorming requires the generation of as many unusual or creative ideas as possible from lots of different angles. So don't worry too much about the practicality of your ideas – just try to think up as many as possible. You'd be surprised how many seemingly impractical ideas can be worked up, refined and made workable later.

How many Brainstorm *problems would I have to tackle at an assessment centre?*

Probably between six to eight.

As there are no right or wrong answers, how can I judge my performance?

Read the self-review guidelines, after the end of Test 28 *Brainstorm 3*. After you have completed the self review, you might like to ask a friend or relative to have a go, and then compare the two sets of answers. They may generate other possibilities that you haven't even thought of.

What if I'm not a very creative person?

If you've never tried this type of test before, you could find it challenging. This is not the sort of skill you ever learnt at school. However, in this test, experience, knowledge and confidence are just as important as creativity, so give it a go – you could surprise yourself.

In fact, the most difficult thing about it is coming up with the first few ideas. You might have trouble on the first test, but then as you work your way through the others you'll notice how your creative ideas begin to flow. It's a little bit like turning on a tap; the water trickles out to begin with, then flows faster and faster.

You can always come back to the tests for another try. The first time I tried a *Brainstorm* test I only managed 3 decent ideas. The second time I thought up 26. So try the tests and watch your creativity catch fire.

Instructions for Tests 26, 27 and 28

Instructions: Each *Brainstorm* test contains a different problem. In each case, depending on the wording of the question, you are required either to give as many explanations as you can why the problem has occurred, or to suggest as many solutions as possible.

If this is not your book then I suggest you write out your answers on a separate piece of paper. When writing out your answers, keep your writing legible. In a real live test the test administrator can't award you any marks unless he or she can read your writing!

Time guideline: Allow yourself 4 minutes for each test. This will give you a realistic feel for the time you will be given when you take the real thing.

Test 26 Brainstorm 1

You are the Marketing Manager of an organisation that is planning to open up a new health club and gym on a greenfield site on the outskirts of a town.

List as many ways as you can to publicise this new venture to attract new members to get the gym off to a good start. The instructions are given on the previous page.

1 _____

2 _____

3 _____

4 _____

5 _____

6 _____

7 _____

8 _____

9 _____

10 _____

11 _____

12 _____

13 _____

14 _____

15 _____

16 _____

17 _____

18 _____

19 _____

20 _____

Test 27 Brainstorm 2

Here is another *Brainstorm* for you to try. The instructions and time guideline are printed before on page 123.

You are the Managing Director of a company with a small IT helpdesk that is responsible for supporting the IT needs of the rest of the organisation. You are having significant difficulties retaining people in this role. They tend to leave after a couple of months just as they start to become productive.

List as many possible reasons as you can for the high staff turnover in this function:

1 _____

2 _____

3 _____

4 _____

5 _____

6 _____

7 _____

8 _____

9 _____

10 _____

11 _____

12 _____

13 _____

14 _____

15 _____

16 _____

17 _____

18 _____

19 _____

20 _____

Test 28 Brainstorm 3

Here is another *Brainstorm* for you to try which I think is rather fun. The instructions and time guideline are printed on page 123.

You arrive at work expecting to give a detailed presentation to your boss and other senior managers only to discover the paperwork, which you have been preparing for the last three weeks, is securely locked inside your desk. What do you do?

1 _____

2 _____

3 _____

4 _____

5 _____

6 _____

7 _____

8 _____

9 _____

10 _____

11 _____

12 _____

13 _____

14 _____

15 _____

16 _____

17 _____

18 _____

19 _____

20 _____

Self-review for the brainstorm tests

Brainstorming requires people to generate as many unusual or creative ideas as possible that can be refined and made practical later. Work your way through the following self-review questions and use these to help you to focus on what you must do when you take the test for real:

◆ How did you find the time pressure? Four minutes is not very long so you need to be quick, and not dwell too long on each answer. Try to generate as many different answers as you can in the time.

◆ How legible are your answers? Although you need to work quickly, your answers will be read by an assessor. Feel free to write in short note format, but make sure it is comprehensible to someone else.

◆ How creative were you? One of the secrets of brainstorming is to generate as many ideas and from as many different angles as you can. Do not worry too much about the practicality of them – this happens later.

◆ Did you read the question carefully? One example asked you for suggestions for solving the problem and the other asked you for explanations of it. You need to ensure that your answers were appropriate in each case.

◆ Once you have completed the self-review you might like to ask a friend, colleague or relative to have a go, and then compare your answers. This may generate other possibilities that you had not contemplated.

Now you have taken the brainstorm tests and worked through the self-review, you should feel much more comfortable with this type of test should you encounter it during your job search. You know what to expect, you've had some valuable practice, so you should feel a lot more confident as a result.

Test 29 *Fastrack*

Fastrack is a card-based test measuring problem-solving and analysis aptitude. In other words, it tests how you think.

In order to successfully complete this test you will have to:

◆ Understand the problem you are presented with.
◆ Identify information relating to the problem.
◆ Identify patterns within this information.
◆ Generate the correct strategy to solve the problem.
◆ Apply this strategy and decide on the answers to the problem in question.

Like all the tests in this chapter, *Fastrack* is used to assess graduates for management and junior management roles, especially those requiring analytical and problem-solving skills. The only difference between this test and the real thing is that at an assessment centre you'll probably be given five different problems to tackle instead of one.

Test 29 does not require the use of a calculator, however please note some *Fastrack* tests do require one.

Instructions: On the opposite page you will see 10 boxes (at the assessment centre these will be made of card). The first box marked Situation P contains instructions, the rest contain information. The information in two of the boxes is incomplete.

It is your job to look at the boxes with complete information, work out the underlying rules and patterns, then complete the missing information in the spaces provided on the two answer sheets. If you cannot reach a decision, mark your best choice but avoid wild guessing.

Note: It may be helpful to photocopy the page, so that you can then cut out the 10 boxes and spread them out on a desk in front of you, re-ordering them as you wish (due to copyright restrictions please only photocopy this book for your own use).

Once you have made a decision as to the answers to the questions, check them by comparing them to the correct answers on page 130.

Time guideline: Once you're happy that you know exactly what you're expected to do, allow yourself 7 minutes to work on the actual problem.

Test 29 Answer Sheet

Tick the relevant box to indicate whether the Priority Code should be High or Low:

CARD Priority Code

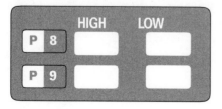

Indicate the Machine Time in hours:

CARD Machine Time

P   SITUATION P   *INSTRUCTION CARD*

PAA Foods plc manufacturers 'own-brand' cleaning products for supermarkets.
Cards P1–P9 represent outstanding orders from clients.
Based on the completed cards, establish the priority codes and machine times where they are missing.
Mark your answers in the Answer Sheet section.

P 1   MONDAY 24 HourStores

Order Quantity	32,000 units
Previous Orders	200,000 units
Process Code	P106
Priority Code	LOW
Machine Time	8 hrs

P 2   MONDAY   Cambridge Provisions

Order Quantity	30,000 units
Previous Orders	75,000 units
Process Code	Y654
Priority Code	LOW
Machine Time	10 hrs

P 3   TUESDAY Brook Ltd

Order Quantity	12,000 units
Previous Orders	450,000 units
Process Code	Y654
Priority Code	HIGH
Machine Time	4 hrs

P 4   TUESDAY   HYY Stores

Order Quantity	12,000 units
Previous Orders	350,000 units
Process Code	Y654
Priority Code	LOW
Machine Time	4 hrs

P 5   MONDAY Chaundry & Sons Ltd

Order Quantity	16,000 units
Previous Orders	450,000 units
Process Code	P106
Priority Code	HIGH
Machine Time	4 hrs

P 6   TUESDAY Kent and Co

Order Quantity	32,000 units
Previous Orders	400,000 units
Process Code	J765
Priority Code	HIGH
Machine Time	4 hrs

P 7   WEDNESDAY Cook & Watson Ltd

Order Quantity	32,000 units
Previous Orders	400,000 units
Process Code	P106
Priority Code	HIGH
Machine Time	8 hrs

P 8   THURSDAY Saver Stores

Order Quantity	48,000 units
Previous Orders	250,000 units
Process Code	P106
Priority Code	?
Machine Time	?

P 9   THURSDAY Poundright

Order Quantity	6,000 units
Previous Orders	200,000 units
Process Code	Y654
Priority Code	?
Machine Time	?

Answers are given on the next page.

Answers to Test 29

The answers include an explanation for how they were reached, which you might find very useful for understanding the thought process that goes into the making of the *Fastrack* test.

CARD Priority Code

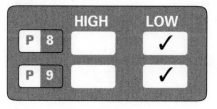

In order to establish the missing Priority Codes it would have been useful to order the cards into two columns in front of you, one column for High Priority Codes and the other for Low Priority Codes.

When the Previous Orders are 400,000 units and above the Priority Code is High.

For Previous Orders of less than 400,000 the Priority Code is Low.

CARD Machine Time

P	8	12 Hours
P	9	2 Hours

In order to establish the missing Machine Times it would have been useful to re-order the cards into two columns, one for Process Code Y654 and the other for Process Code P106 (card P6, Process Code J765, is irrelevant).

For Process Code P106 you can see that for an order quantity of 32,000 units the machine time is 8 hours and for 16,000 units the machine time is 4 hours.

The rule here is that for Process Code P106 it takes 1 hour for every 4,000 units.

For Process Code Y654 you can see that for an order quantity of 30,000 units the machine time is 10 hours and for 12,000 units the machine time is 4 hours.

The rule here is that for Process Code Y654 it takes 1 hour for every 3,000 units.

The *Scenarios* tests

Scenarios is a 'paper and pencil' test designed to assess an individual's understanding of everyday management situations, as well as the effectiveness of the individual's responses to these situations. In other words, your managerial judgement.

Companies who use it want to know whether you have the basic knowledge and know-how to make an effective and successful manager.

Knowing how to manage, however, is not exactly the same thing as *actually* managing – for this companies use personality questionnaires such as the *OPQ* and also assess your performance during management exercises (see Chapter 10).

Like all the tests in this chapter, *Scenarios* is used to assess graduates for management and junior management roles, especially those requiring analytical and problem-solving skills.

Time guideline: There is no time limit for the completion of the two *Scenario* example questions, however allowing yourself around three minutes for each one will encourage you to work quickly and prevent you pondering too long on any one item. But don't set the clock until you've read the instructions (below) and familiarised yourself with the rating scale.

Instructions: First of all have a good look at the rating scale printed below.

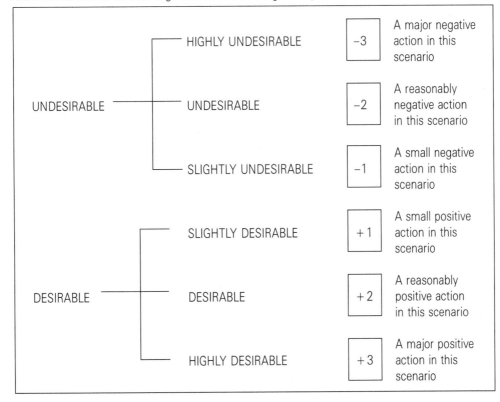

Now read the text of the first *Scenario* problem and the five different response options listed underneath. For each response option, decide whether you think it is an undesirable or desirable course of action. Once you have made up your mind about that, decide exactly *how* undesirable or desirable the option is, as per the rating scale shown above.

For example, if you think the response option is an extremely good idea, give it the highest rating of +3. If you think it's a terrible idea, give it a –3. You can, of course, choose any of the ratings in-between those two extremes.

Note your answers down on a piece of paper, then have a go at the second scenarios test. Then read my explanation, which will give you a pretty good idea if your answers are, from a business and management point of view, in the right ball park or not.

Please note there is no answer sheet to fill in. Because of the complexity of this test, I felt it would be better to explain how to go about tackling it. But in the live *Scenarios* test, you will be given the usual psychometric test-type answer sheet complete with lots of little circles to fill in.

Test 30 *Scenario* 1

You have just been promoted to run a department which was reputedly well managed and highly effective under your predecessor. She has subsequently been promoted to a new post within the organisation in another part of the country.

During your initial few months you would:

1   Personally conduct an immediate and critical review of all existing departmental policies and practices.

2   Inform your staff that you will be making no major changes to the department for at least 6 months.

3   Ask your staff for ideas on how to make further improvements to the department.

4   Write an article on your department's aims and objectives in a local business journal.

5   Get involved in several interdepartmental project teams as a means of getting to know your management peers.

Test 31 *Scenario 2*

You supervise a team of 6 people and are responsible for overseeing their work on a daily basis. Your immediate manager is generally happy with your performance, but has voiced concerns over your recent scheduling of overtime. Specifically she wonders why overtime is invariably necessary on a Friday afternoon. You have explained that workload is very heavy with just six staff and there is an urgent need to ensure work is completed before the weekend – otherwise customer delays will result. Your manager is not convinced and has asked you only to schedule paid overtime after direct consultation with her.

However, the following Friday a fault has developed with your customer systems which, although rectified four hours later, has caused considerable mayhem to your team's schedule. If the backlog is not cleared, you know there will be irate customers next week. Several of your team offer to stay on to address the backlog but if you allow this, overtime pay will be necessary. However, your manager and others at a comparable level have gone to an off-site meeting and cannot be contacted.

You would:

1   Schedule the paid overtime and deal with the consequences later.

2   Respect your manager's decision and send your team home with a view to tackling the situation on Monday morning.

3   Explain to the staff that this is a team problem and therefore everyone needs to remain behind and work unpaid overtime.

4   Send your team home but stay on yourself for a few hours to salvage what you can from the situation.

5   Have a brief report of your reasons for scheduling paid overtime on your manager's desk before her return on Monday.

Test 32 *Scenario* 3

You manage a small team within your organisation. One member of the team has been working on an important business issue (on his own initiative), and has come up with a proposal, which he would like to present at a meeting of staff from other teams and departments. He has asked you for support for the proposal, but you believe his idea to be unsound. Please rate the following possible courses of action:

1 Agree to support him but then find an excuse for not attending the meeting.

2 Tell him you will make up your mind on the proposal after listening to the discussion at the meeting.

3 Point out the weaknesses of the proposal but encourage him to try again.

4 Tell him it is impractical/too costly/not the right time and encourage him to withdraw the proposal for the time being.

5 Ask him to discuss the proposal informally with other colleagues before scheduling the meeting.

Test 33 *Scenario* 4

You lead a team of individuals, which relies on the use of computer systems and data banks in carrying out its daily workload. Following a major reorganisation, a number of your important procedures and work systems have been radically altered. Many of your old systems and methods have been replaced with new ones. In addition, you and your team will be required to work in a closer fashion with a neighbouring departmental team. There are rumours that the teams may merge within the year.

New systems are now in place which need to be mastered by you and your staff before the work of your team can be successfully conducted; these systems will be used on a daily basis.

You are considering a number of possible strategies to ensure the smooth changeover from old systems to new. It is important that any disruption to the smooth running of your team's work is kept to a minimum throughout the changeover. Please rate the following possible strategies:

1   Encourage your team to start trying to use the new systems, reverting to the old systems over the coming weeks only under time pressure.

2   Set up a small project team comprising members of your team and the other department to handle the changeover.

3   Continue to utilise the old systems; wait until there is a quiet period in your team's work schedule and then have everyone trained in the new system.

4   Personally draft a comprehensive report detailing the new systems and circulate it around your team.

5   Rearrange your team's priorities to ensure that training in the new systems is given as soon as possible to staff who will use the systems the most.

As mentioned above, I have not given you an answer sheet to fill in because I want to give you a little more explanation, and in any case there are no real right or wrong answers since the degree of positive or negative will always vary between people. My intention is to help you understand the thinking behind the test. So if your answers are basically similar to mine, you'll know you're on the right track.

Scenarios 1

1   This response is probably not a good idea. It could be argued that this response is an obvious choice for a new manager getting to know his department. However, I think the word 'critical' implies that you might be seen to be raring to make changes just for the sake of it. This could alienate staff and even be perceived as quite threatening. Therefore I'd give this a low rating, probably a –3.

2   Informing staff you will not be making any changes is another bad idea. A lot can happen in six months, and it would be a foolish manager who promised otherwise. I'd give this a –2 or a –3.

3   Asking staff for suggestions on how to improve things is a good idea. I would have preferred the question to have been worded slightly differently, because *only* asking for improvements could be seen as a criticism. However, as you have no choice but to work with the given wording, I'd still award this a +2.

4   As a new manager, writing an article in the local paper would surely be totally inappropriate at this early stage. Therefore I'd give this response a low rating, probably a –2 or a –3.

5   Getting involved would be a good way to learn what makes your department tick. If you got to know your management peers as a result, that would also be a bonus. Therefore I'd give this response a high rating, probably a +3.

Scenarios 2

1   The way I see it, you have *got* to get the work done for the sake of the company. Therefore this response must be awarded a high score, say +2 or +3, even though there may be hell to pay on Monday. Personally I'd prefer the response option to read, '*Schedule the paid overtime and buy your manager a mobile phone,*' but it doesn't.

2   My immediate reaction to this was that surely the right answer depends on the culture and ethos of the company in question. Then I realised that managers are paid to make tricky decisions, and clearly waiting until Monday would be disastrous. Therefore I'd give this response the lowest rating possible, –3.

3   This could create a lot of bad will. Why should anyone be forced to work late on a Friday evening for nothing? Good managers are considerate and reasonable, therefore I would give this a very low rating, perhaps a –3.

4   Considering what needs to be done is at least a six-man job, how much could you realistically expect to achieve by yourself? Not much. However, I suppose it would be better than doing nothing, so I'd give this response a +1, but no higher.

5   This is perhaps the best idea of all. You salvage the situation, keep your staff happy *and* explain your actions, hopefully pre-empting any criticism.

Scenarios 3

1   I give this a – 3. I think it's a very bad idea because it will create bad will and mistrust and it shirks responsibility.

2   I give this a + 2 because it may be that other people will have useful feedback and ideas (or ideas to make the proposal work) that you haven't considered.

3   I give this a + 2 because I think it's good to have an frank and honest discussion and to encourage employees.

4   I give this a – 2 because it could create bad will and could be seen as dismissive and uncaring.

5   I give this a – 2 because I don't think its a good idea to get the whole office discussing something you have already decided you don't want. It would be a waste of time.

Scenarios 4

1   I give this a + 2 because everyone has to start using the systems sometime, it might as

well be now. Using the old systems to help them through busy patches will keep your department on target.

2   I give this a + 1 (not a negative) – quite good for communication, but on the other hand it might mean vital staff are away discussing the 'problem' when you need all the manpower you can get.

3   I give this a − 3. I don't think the quiet period will ever happen, and you need to start using new systems now. If you don't you could get very behind and nobody will have learnt anything.

4   It's good to give people clear information so they all know what's going on and how to proceed so + 1 or + 2.

5   I give this a + 2 because I think that getting people trained up as soon as possible is a very good idea

Four more things you should know about Scenarios

◆ Firstly, in the live test, you will be given a psychometric test-type answer sheet complete with lots of little circles to fill in.

◆ Next, when taking the *Scenarios* cenarios test, resist the temptation to give alternative answers. I have to admit that when confronted with *Scenarios* for the first time I felt like scribbling, 'It's impossible to answer this question,' but that would not have helped. You *must* follow the instructions, and rate each response option as per the rating scale.

◆ The same goes for explaining your reasons, or changing the wording of the response options. *Only* consider and rate the choices given, and *only* fill in the answer sheet according to the instructions.

◆ Don't worry if you find some of the response options difficult to rate. Pick something (never miss out a question) and move on. In a live *Scenarios* test you will have – wait for it – up to 100 responses to rate! This is a good thing. It's your performance over the entire test which counts, not any one particular answer.

◆ Finally, a tip from SHL themselves: try to be decisive. A good manager will either reject an idea, or go for it, not sit on the fence. I'm not advising you to avoid the middling scores of –1 and +1 completely, I'm merely suggesting you avoid picking them 100% of the time.

The next chapter concentrates on the most popular management exercises such as presentations, in-tray exercises, group discussions etc.

Management tests and exercises – how to improve your performance is also covered at the end of **Chapter Ten**.

Management Exercises

Whereas the previous chapter covered specific management tests, this chapter is concerned with the most popular types of management exercise, including:

◆ presentations
◆ in-tray exercises
◆ one-on-one role plays
◆ group exercises
◆ physical activities and group tasks
◆ interviews.

Presentations, in-tray exercises and one-on-one role-plays are all examples of **individual exercises** where you will find yourself under the spotlight and being assessed according to your individual performance. What's important here is management style and know-how because all these exercises are designed to 'simulate' the different and varied activities commonly performed by managers.

Group discussions and physical activities are both forms of **group exercise.** Generally your ability to interact well with other people is what's being assessed here.

You will encounter some, but rarely all, of these types of exercise during your assessment centre visit (or as you progress along a large organisation's recruitment process), especially if you are aiming for any sort of management or trainee management position. In fact, the higher up the corporate ladder you're aiming, the more rigorous the testing process...until you get to board level. For some strange reason, potential company directors are not always subjected to such close scrutiny.

If it sounds tough – it's supposed to. Some management exercises, particularly presentations, can be particularly stressful, and by the end of the assessment centre you'll probably feel totally worn out. However, it's worth remembering that for the recruiting organisation, the administration of every assessment centre and every management exercise is time-consuming and extremely costly. Therefore you can be assured that the numbers of candidates who reach this stage will have been kept to a minimum and that the organisation in question is obviously taking you and your appointment seriously. In other words, it may be tough but at least you're on the short list!

Presentations

Presentations are extremely popular with employers recruiting into management positions. Here you are expected to talk to an audience on a given subject for approximately 10 minutes, with or without advanced preparation. The audience will consist of one or more people from the recruiting organisation and very occasionally, other candidates as well.

For many people giving a presentation can be the most traumatic part of the assessment centre, probably because of anxieties about your performance under the spotlight. If this sounds like you, you're not alone. Public speaking is a daunting prospect for most people, even those who do it on a regular basis. The following FAQ, ideas and tips should help, and who knows - you might even enjoy it!

How likely is it that I will be asked to make a presentation?

Very likely indeed. Expect to be asked to give a presentation when applying for any management job, from graduate trainee right up to the most senior positions.

How long should my presentation last?

The presentation itself will not normally be expected to last more than 10 minutes; 20 at the absolute maximum. The recruiting organisation will always tell you exactly what you're expected to do. If necessary, you can cut your presentation slightly short of the required time, but *never overrun*.

How much notice will I be given?

If you're told you will be expected to give a presentation when you attend an assessment centre, then anything from a few days' to several weeks' notice. If the presentation is sprung on you after you arrive, you'll usually be given up to an hour to prepare.

Will I be given any material to assist me in my preparation?

If you're given the title of your presentation in advance, then no. Organisations don't usually allow their internal assessment material out into the public domain. However, if the presentation is sprung on you on the day, it's possible you could be given a pack of business-type information on which you will be expected to base your presentation.

Will I have to stand on a 'stage' under a spotlight?

You could be expected to 'perform' standing up, in front of several assessors and possibly other candidates as well, but thankfully the most modern approach is for candidates to present to just one or two people from the recruiting organisation, with everyone sitting around a desk.

What subject will I be given?

Subjects relevant to the recruiting organisation's business or industry are very popular. For example, say you are applying to a company in the airline industry, your subject could easily be something very general such as, *'In your opinion, what's going to happen to the airline industry in the 21st Century?'*

Alternatively they could ask you to discuss a specific issue relevant to the industry. You might be given a press cutting on the issue and then instructed to argue for or against the opinions expressed in the article. This type of scenario is quite common where companies are looking for candidates with particular background knowledge.

Often a subject will be slanted towards the actual position you are applying for. For example, say you were applying for a management position running a graduate recruitment programme, you might be asked to talk about, *'Your strategy for ensuring you recruited the very best candidates ahead of the competition.'*

Obviously the recruiting organisation would be hoping you'd put some serious thought into how *you* would run the graduate programme, should they offer you the job. Could you come up with sensible, workable ideas? Have you considered the problems and challenges of the position? Have you thought about it seriously at all?

On the other hand, and especially for more general management positions, your presentation topic might concern any one of a whole multitude of business-related issues. Say you've applied for a senior management position in a large retail superstore, you might be asked to present on something like the following:

- The likely impact on your sales when a competitor opens up nearby.
- Your strategy for maximising sales when the weather is very cold in winter/very hot in summer.
- The impact of a lot of redundancies being made at a nearby factory.
- How you would deal with disruption caused by the store going through a refit.
- How you would deal with disruption at the store caused by the car park being resurfaced.

◆ How you would deal with a competitor at national level making major changes to its pricing structure.

◆ The impact of a new point-of-sale IT system.

Obviously there are thousands of other similar topics that could come up, but you get the picture.

Some organisations prefer to steer clear of industry-related topics, instead opting for one of the interests or hobbies you've listed on your CV. This is a very popular choice. So don't claim to be a champion ballroom dancer unless you really are.

Another possibility, and possibly the hardest, is being asked to choose your own subject, when the most articulate person's mind can go completely and utterly blank. Be warned – canny candidates often carry prepared notes in their briefcase, just in case this happens. Why not be one of them?

The following section explains the basics of presentation preparation.

Preparing your presentation

The following sections cover business-related and non-business related presentation topics, however the ideas they contain are really applicable to both. So I suggest you read both sections and use whichever ideas you like the most.

1. Business-related topics – research and brainstorm your ideas

Depending upon your given subject, you may first need to do a little research. **Chapter Eight** will give you lots of ideas on how to do this, unless, of course, you are already thoroughly conversant with the relevant industry and the issues which concern it.

If your subject is **business-related** the recruiting organisation will no doubt be looking at your managerial style and know-how. Assuming that if you succeed in landing the job you'll probably be given a certain amount of autonomy to make decisions and possibly a budget to spend, they'll want to know what you'd do with it.

Faced with the problems/situations as described in the business-related examples given above, can you demonstrate an understanding of the issues involved? Can you come up with sensible, workable ideas? Are you capable of devising a good business strategy to deal with problems? Can you even find ways of taking advantage of a situation?

Here are some examples using the scenario given above (you're applying for a senior position at a large retail superstore) of some of the things you could consider including in your presentation:

'*Your strategy for maximising sales when the weather is very cold in winter.*'
–   Grit the car park so customers don't slip on black ice.
–   Help people/the elderly/disabled, and their shopping, to their cars.
–   Minimise the distance people have to walk in inclement weather to collect/dispose of their trolley.
–   Warm customers up with free hot tea/coffee.
–   Stock plenty of winter-related products, for example, offer a good stock of winter clothing (nothing worse than looking for snow boots and only finding swimwear).

'*How you would deal with disruption at the store caused by the car park being resurfaced.*'
–   Provide large, clear directions for customers looking for a space.
–   Make staff available to direct traffic at the busiest times.
–   Ensure customers are kept well clear of recently tarmaced areas/building works.
–   Meet standards and legal obligations relating to Health and Safety.
–   Schedule the noisiest and most disruptive work away from the busiest shopping periods.

'*The impact of a lot of redundancies being made at a nearby factory.*'
–   Offer cheaper goods/special deals to combat the reduced affluence in the area.
–   Consult your HR people – could this be a good opportunity to pick up some highly qualified and experienced staff?

Can you think of any more? Many of these business scenario-type topics require a good deal of brainstorming, and it would definitely help to have some ideas about which direction you would like to take the job (assuming you land it) and how you would deal with the inevitable challenges it would bring.

Assuming you only have 10 minutes maximum, you can see that you only need three or four items to talk about in some depth. The aim is to show the assessors that you know how to manage.

2. Non business-related topics – deciding what to include

If you've only been given a short time in which to prepare, you're less likely to have to present in depth. In this case the presentation is more a test of your thinking skills and how articulately you present information.

Here you could be asked to present on a topic of your own choice, one of the items you mention on your CV, or something like this: *'Give a 10-minute presentation describing a recent achievement.'*

Let's say you've recently climbed Everest (obviously an 'achievement' could mean anything you wanted), then your first task is to sort out what needs to be included.

Begin by deciding the main points and the principal message you wish to put across to your audience. One way of doing this is to try to sum up your message in one sentence (obviously this also applies to business-related topics).

Then it's time for a bit of brainstorming. Think about the things your audience might be interested in finding out. If you're talking about one of your achievements or a hobby then a good way to do this is to write down a list of approximately 10 questions that an *unenlightened* person might ask. By this I mean, somebody who knows nothing about the subject. For example, as soon as your audience finds out that you're about to speak about your amazing experience of climbing Everest, they'll want to know the following:

- How did you prepare (or train) for the climb?
- What special equipment/clothes did you take?
- Why did you do it?
- Did you follow the tourist trail and employ a team of Sherpas to carry your bags?
- How much did it cost?
- What was the weather like? Any tent-ripping storms etc?
- Any heart-stopping moments?
- What did you do at the summit?
- How long did it take?
- Have you got pictures?
- Which was harder – up or down?

This 'think up about 10 questions' method works really well for any subject but what you must do is **keep it simple**. So for this particular topic, even if you're the world's greatest mountaineering expert – steer clear of the techi stuff. Your audience won't want to be shown hundreds of detailed weather maps, or be lectured on the art of choosing the right socks – they'll just want to hear about what happened when you got lost, or when your climbing buddy fell down a crevasse.

You'll only have about 10 minutes to speak anyway, so **keep it simple.**

If you're *so* steeped in the technical jargon and minute detail of your chosen subject that you're totally incapable of thinking up some basic, obvious, simplistic questions, ask a friend (or even another candidate) to think of them for you.

Your next task is to set about answering all those questions in a logical order. A little bit of information on each item is all that's required – just a few notes to jog your memory. You can see that by setting out the task this way it's not so daunting. Just 10 items to talk about for about a minute each; not so terrible. Or pick the most interesting four or five items – it's up to you.

3. Organise your introduction and ending

The usual recommendation, which I think is very sensible, is to begin by telling your audience who you are and what you are going to tell them. For example: '*I'm Andrea Shavick and today I would like to talk to you about how I climbed Everest, and how I very nearly didn't survive to tell the tale.*'

Your presentation ending should be fairly similar. All you do is sum up the main points again for the audience (in other words, remind the audience about what you've said). Just one or two sentences will suffice. '*So that's how I conquered Everest and lived to tell the tale, despite losing my boots, tent and three fingers.*'

If you want to, it's a nice touch to tag a, '*Has anyone any questions?*' line on the end, and then you're done (although you must be be prepared to answer questions).

4. Writing out your presentation

One very well tried and tested method is to prepare a series of notes on postcard-sized cards. Notes on cards are infinitely better than writing out your presentation in full. You are not giving a speech.

The idea is that you use the cards as a prompt to remind you about the next item on which you are supposed to be speaking, so **only write brief notes on each card**, and **make them legible.** Your audience will not be impressed if you clearly cannot read your own writing!

Remember to **number the cards!**

5. Practise

This really is essential. If you've been busy preparing the presentation at home always try it out on your friends or family, even if it's just to practise talking to an audience without losing your train of thought or having a fit of giggles. People you know and trust are most likely to give you a honest appraisal of your performance, not to mention valuable suggestions.

Another reason to practise is to time yourself. **Never overrun.**

If you haven't been allocated a topic before the big day, prepare some notes on a topic that interests you e.g. one of your hobbies, and practise this instead. As mentioned above, canny candidates often arrive at the assessment centre with a ready-prepared and rehearsed presentation in their briefcase – so why shouldn't you?

6. Props – to use or not to use?

Once you're happy with your general draft, think about delivery. There are lots of audio-visual aids and other props you could use, for example:

◆ overhead projectors
◆ computer programmes like Powerpoint and Excel
◆ video and film
◆ photographs
◆ printed material, including graphs, reports, newspaper cuttings, etc.
◆ objects which could be handed round
◆ flip charts.

If you're interested in using any of these, check with the assessment centre administrator whether or not they will be available. Personally, I think it's better to keep things simple for two important reasons. The first is mainly a matter of confidence. If you're not used to using an overhead projector, now is *not* the time to learn. The last thing you need is for your transparencies to project upside down and in the wrong order. Trust me, the more complicated the prop, the more there is to go wrong.

The second reason is that overuse of audio-visual aids and other high tech props can prove distracting. The recruiting organisation is supposed to be concentrating on *you* and *your ideas*, not your Oscar-winning slide show. *You* are the show, and what you say and how you say it is the important thing.

Therefore only use audio-visual aids or other props that you feel 100% confident with, and only if they're really necessary.

And if you're lacking in the technical wizardry department but still hanker after at least one prop to spice up your presentation, then the good old flip chart can't really be bettered. It's simple, it won't break down, and it won't make you look a complete idiot (unless you trip over the legs).

So you've researched your subject, prepared the presentation, sorted out the props and even practised several times...now what about delivery?

7. Delivering the presentation

Here are a few tips to help you feel confident when just about to begin delivering your presentation:

♦ First of all check that you have all the relevant props, notes etc. close at hand and in the right order.

♦ Then, ditch the drink. If it's not next to you, you can't knock it over!

♦ I am assuming that the assessors will have already introduced you to people from the recruiting organisation, but if you suddenly find yourself asked to present to a group of strangers, ask them who they are and introduce yourself. Be friendly.

♦ Before you launch into your presentation, make sure everyone can hear and see you clearly. Not a problem if you're sitting around a desk, but if you're standing in front of a room of people it won't hurt to enquire, *'Can everyone hear me ok?'*

Whatever you do, remember that you are applying for a managerial position. This means behaving like a manager, i.e. confident and self-assured. So don't blow your chances by immediately announcing to your audience when it's your turn; *'Sorry, I'm really nervous,'* or *'My presentation's not very good,'* or *'Um...I've never given a presentation before,'* because they'll immediately mark you down as a hopeless case before you even begin.

Note: Also see 'Look Smart' which is in **Chapter Seven – Assessment Events and Assessment Centres.**

Now here are some tips to help you keep going once you've begun speaking:

◆ Talk to the audience. Don't talk to the flipchart or bury your nose in your notes. If you look your audience in the eye when you speak they'll not only be able to hear you clearly, they'll stay focused and interested.

◆ Always be professional in your manner. So NO swearing, rude jokes, sexist or racist comments or silly walks.

◆ Once you've got going try to ignore any distractions – there's bound to be something. You can't do anything about roadworks or ringing phones, so it's probably better to accept that they *will* happen and not let them put you off. Only stop for the fire alarm!

◆ People coming into the room or worse, leaving in the middle of your presentation can be especially off-putting. If this happens, pause, say hello to the newcomers and carry on. Always ignore the leavers. Never snap, *'Where do you think you're going?'*

◆ Always stick to your plan. Follow your notes and don't wander off course.

◆ If you're using a flip chart, consider writing down the main points as you go along in big, bold writing, so that everyone in the audience can read what you've written. This helps them remember what you've said, helps them formulate questions to ask you and hopefully, keeps them awake.

◆ Try not to move around too much. Pacing up and down is distracting, as is waving your hands about all the time.

◆ With business-related topics and just one or two assessors sitting around a table – they may not be able to resist interrupting your flow and pitching in with a few ideas of their own (or questions about something you've said). If your presentation turns into a discussion, go with the flow. Move on once the discussion has come to an end.

- Be prepared to for a sudden attack of the shakes right in the middle of your presentation. This is completely normal and can affect the most confident, well-prepared person. If this happens to you, pause, smile at your audience, take a deep breath...and carry on.

- Although you'll be concentrating on your own performance, watch out for your audience's body language too. An unacceptable level of fidgeting or coughing probably means they're bored. If this happens, consider cutting short any long-winded explanations, or try to get a move on with winding up your presentation completely. If you hear any snoring...

- Once you've finished the presentation, smile and ask your audience whether they have any questions and **be prepared to answer them**. You've just climbed Everest, what are you going to try next? Why do you want to work in a boring office when you obviously lead such an exciting life? If you really have just climbed Everest, do you have a good answer?

- At the end, just before you sit down, thank your audience for their time.

- Smile.

- Whatever happens, try to enjoy yourself. If your presentation goes well, I guarantee you'll wish you could have gone on for longer. But don't. There's always someone who overruns – make sure it isn't you.

As with group role-plays and exercises, giving a presentation will put you under considerable pressure – and I'm afraid that's the intention. Remember that all the other candidates will be feeling just as nervous as you, so if you are ever in the situation where you're part of *their* audience, give them your support and encouragement.

In-tray exercises

The in-tray exercise (sometimes called an *in-basket exercise*) is another very popular management test which you are likely to encounter during your assessment centre appointment.

To begin with you will be given some general background information about a hypothetical company and details of your job role in that company, for example, marketing manager.

Then you will be told about a situation in which you have to imagine yourself, such as:

'You are a marketing manager for our company. It is 3pm, and in two hours' time you will be leaving for a week's holiday. However you still have 15 items in your in-tray which need tackling. Put the 15 items in priority order, and then explain your reasons in writing.'

Or the scenario could be simpler:

'At work you have a number of things to do. Prioritise the different tasks, explaining your reasons in writing.'

Now for the fun part. You will be handed, in random order, a number of items which supposedly have been taken out of your hypothetical 'in-tray'. Typical items will include:

◆ faxes
◆ memos
◆ correspondence
◆ emails
◆ notes
◆ telephone/voicemail messages.

Each one will say where it's come from – a customer, a supplier, a member of staff, another manager, the MD, perhaps an outside agency such as a government official or a health and safety inspector etc., and sometimes what you're supposed to do with it. A growing trend is to hand you a bundle of *real* correspondence taken from a manager's in-tray.

Your job is to prioritise all the items and decide which ones to tackle first, second, third and so on, giving reasons as to why you made each decision. You will also be expected to decide the appropriate course of action to be taken in each case. All this must be written down in a legible, understandable way.

There are no right or wrong answers to this exercise. It's all a matter of personal managerial style.

Note: Your in-tray correspondence may be delivered to you on a PC in MS Outlook, Lotus Notes or similar.

What's the point of the exercise?

Basically to see how you would deal with the numerous pressing issues that managers are presented with on a daily basis. The in-tray exercise is a 'real work' simulation – the assessors are primarily interested in seeing whether your decisions make sound business sense or not. The ability to prioritise, evaluate, make good business decisions and work under pressure are all necessary management skills.

Furthermore, because you are usually expected to present your reasons for each decision in writing, your written communication skills are also being tested.

Why do I have to explain my decisions in writing?

Asking you to explain your reasons in writing is intended to prevent candidates picking the order of items at random without giving the issues involved and individual problems any thought. It also allows the recruiting organisation to assess (or 'mark') your in-tray exercise later in the day.

Don't worry about having to write down your answers – nobody's expecting you to write a book on the subject. A numbered list with brief explanations next to each one will be sufficient. Make sure your writing's legible.

Are in-tray exercises ever taken alongside other candidates?

You will usually work on an in-tray exercise by yourself. Sometimes a manager from the recruiting organisation will sit next to you and act as a kind of sounding board, and very occasionally you'll find yourself working alongside other candidates in a group. There are no rules – it's up to the assessors to decide how best to run the exercise.

How long will the exercise take?

Around one to two hours in total. This may sound like a long time, but time flies when you're under pressure and faced with say, 20 items to deal with before the deadline passes.

What should I do first?

Before diving straight in, first spend some time carefully reading the information you've been given about the hypothetical company; this should give you some clues about what sort of issues are particularly important to them.

Next, carefully read any instructions you've been given on tackling the exercise or presenting your answers. For example, you might be instructed to draft replies to certain items of correspondence. If this is the case you really need to know about it at the beginning of your time, not five minutes before the end.

Then read each in-tray item thoroughly, making a quick list and noting down ideas that occur to you next to each one. Possibly you could give each item a rating out of 10 for importance and another rating out of 10 for urgency. What you're doing is formulating a plan, evaluating and analysing all the information before actually committing yourself to anything.

What sort of things need to be taken into consideration?

For each item there will be a number of issues to consider. In no particular order, these are:

♦ **Where the item/letter/email etc. originated.**
How important is the contact? Are they a valued customer or supplier? Are they somebody at the top of the organisation such as the managing director, or another equally important decision-maker? Has the item come from an outside source, such as the press, a trade union or government? The more important the contact, the more priority it should be given.

♦ **The importance of the specific item.**
How important do you think the item is to the company? For example, an item concerning an imminent visit from health and safety inspectors who have the power to close down your entire manufacturing plant should definitely be treated with rather more urgency than, say, a letter concerning the repair of the coffee machine. A serious complaint from a very large customer should perhaps be dealt with before booking the firm's Christmas party, and so on.

◆ **The time frame**.

Here, you need to think about the urgency of each individual item, and what the consequences might be if you delayed taking any action. How long ago was the item sent? Do you still have time to respond or take action? Is there a deadline that can't be missed i.e. latest accounts filing date or two million bananas in the warehouse approaching their sell-by date? Can you negotiate an extension?

For non-urgent items, can you get somebody to call the person concerned and assure them their enquiry/complaint etc. is being dealt with? This won't take long and is better than nothing. Remember that no matter how trivial *you* feel a piece of correspondence is, the person who sent it will not agree with you.

◆ **The consequences of not tackling the task in question at all**.

This should also be considered. Sometimes not doing something seemingly trivial can have serious repercussions.

After this you'll need to decide *how* to deal with each item. By this I mean whether you want to tackle the item yourself or delegate it to somebody else. You would delegate jobs where there's either somebody more appropriate or better qualified to deal with the item than you, or where you want to free up your own time to deal with more pressing matters.

Note: Watch out for items that relate in some way to each other, with one needing sorting out before you can begin the next, or a situation in which tackling item Y means you can't action item Z. Organisations just love adding these neat little touches to see how you respond.

Are there other popular items which could be included?

Yes. Bearing in mind you're applying for managerial positions, then **staffing issues** are very popular, especially items relating to attendance or performance. Sorting this sort of thing out can be time-consuming and can't always be delegated.

Is there anything I should avoid when making my decisions?

The trick is to decide which tasks are the most important to the business and put those ones at the top of your list. Whatever you do don't pick items simply because they're easy, quick, or sound like fun. It's human nature to do this, but try to resist.

Also, don't give priority or allocate much time to items that are only relevant to you personally – such as a message from your neighbour to say your washing machine's flooding! Allocate one minute to phone a plumber, then get back on track with the more pressing managerial issues.

Finally, when deciding how to deal with each in-tray item, remember that as a manager you can always delegate jobs to other people in your hypothetical organisation. Don't attempt everything yourself. Delegating the less important tasks will leave you free to concentrate on the vitally important ones, making better use of your time as a manager.

One-on-one role plays

In this type of exercise the recruiting organisation presents you with some sort of typical business situation which you are then expected to act out with you playing the role of the manager.

There will always be two other people involved – one playing an 'opposing' role, and the other sitting quietly in the corner observing and assessing your performance. This quiet observer will be an experienced manager from the recruiting company who will decide whether to offer you a job based on your performance (as well as your performance in psychometric tests, interviews and other exercises).

The most popular scenario is that you (as manager) are asked to deal with a member of your staff concerning some sort of performance issue. This is because

a) in a management role you will often have to do just that, and

b) staff problems, as opposed to say, customer problems, are usually the trickiest to deal with.

Here's an example:
'You are a manager and you have a meeting with a member of your team who is not performing. What do you do?'

Maybe your staff member has been turning in sub-standard work lately, maybe they've been calling in sick on the same day each week or they keep coming in late. Your job is to talk to that person about the issue, get to the root of the problem and hopefully resolve the issue satisfactorily.

As you can see, this is yet another 'simulation' of a real business situation, but this time it's your ability to deal with people that's being assessed.

Remember that as a manager, staff issues are something that you'll have to deal with on a regular basis – the recruiting organisation quite reasonably wants to see how effective you are at it.

As well as treating people who may be subordinate to you with respect and empathy, you also have a business or a department or team to run. So not only do you have to get to the bottom of the problem but you will also be expected to negotiate a strategy or solution that meets both the member of staff's needs and those of the business. You also have to finish up with your staff member respecting you too – not vowing to walk out because you've acted so unreasonably. Sometimes this can be a tough balancing act, even for the most experienced manager.

Other scenarios might involve a role-play between you and an important customer or perhaps a valued supplier or business partner. You might have to discuss one of any number of business situations such as a change in your packaging requirements or pricing structure.

In all these cases, and in every single role-play, the entire scenario is designed extremely carefully. You can be assured the person playing the staff member or disgruntled supplier will know their lines off by heart. *The only person in the room ad-libbing is you!*

The other thing I need to warn you about is that although you'll be given a certain amount of information before the role-play begins, there's bound to be something thrown into the conversation that you know nothing about. This is entirely deliberate – it's set up in order to see how you'll react. So if you're asked to role-play, expect the unexpected.

Group exercises

Group exercises are timed discussions, where a group of participants work together to tackle a work-related problem. You are observed by assessors, who are not looking for right or wrong answers, but at how you interact with your colleagues in the team.

There are various different types of group exercise. Sometimes all participants are assigned a specific role to play. You might all be told something like this:

You are the Board of Directors of XYZ company and you are planning to move premises to either ABC or DEF location – discuss the impact of this decision.

Although the group as a whole will be given various pieces of information to help the discussion along, each of you will be allocated a certain role to play. For example, one of you could be instructed to take on the role of finance director, another could be marketing director, another could be HR director, and so on. Each of you will be expected to negotiate from your own perspective.

Another popular scenario is where you are all given a different company or departments to represent, all of which want to secure money from a central fund. You might be instructed to hold a board meeting to decide how much to allocate to each company or departments, with everyone arguing their case.

Usually you will be given helpful information that will assist you. If you take the example given above, then the criteria for allocating funds will be clearly spelt out.

Yet another example might be that you are all told that you are members of a marketing team for a pharmaceutical company. The team might then be asked to discuss the launch of a new consumer product, covering issues such as advertising, ethical concerns, packaging and pricing.

With this scenario everyone has the same brief and nobody is assigned to lead the discussion. The assessors are looking for your individual contribution to the team as well as your verbal communication and planning skills.

HR professionals sometimes refer to these group exercises as *assigned role* or *non-assigned role* exercises. In an assigned role exercise each participant plays a different part. In a non-assigned exercise, everyone is given the same brief.

Note: Often the company running the assessment centre will have prepared a range of exercises with a specific industry in mind. For example, if you're after a management position in finance, the exercises could all be based around a fictitious building society or bank. If you're in the manufacturing business, your assessment centre exercises could be based around a hypothetical company which manufactures popular consumer goods, or food.

Rather than sitting around a table, you could be asked to carry out a **physical task** together with some of the other candidates. Be prepared for this, especially if you are aiming for a position involving technical ability. Tasks can include:

◆ building Lego models
◆ designing and building 3-dimensional vehicles
◆ business games
◆ treasure hunts.

By putting you in this situation, the organisation can clearly see how well you get on with other people, whether you consider other people's views, what your teamwork's like, how you cope under pressure, what position you assume in the group, whether you're willing to compromise, if you can conjure up relevant and creative ideas, whether you get involved or sit on the sidelines...the list is endless.

The trick is to try to ignore the observers sitting on the sidelines scribbling silently into their notebooks and try to enjoy yourself. It *is* a very pressurised situation, but remember all the other candidates will be feeling the same way as you. Whatever you do, always be considerate towards the other candidates. *Never* rubbish another person's opinion however ridiculous it is, and don't get into an argument.

Why do so many employers use group exercises as an assessment tool?

One reason employers use group discussions and exercises to assess candidates is because they need people who can work in teams, influence others and demonstrate some degree of interpersonal sensitivity. It's not enough to simply pass all the psychometric tests, you need real managerial skills as well. Participating in a group exercise enables candidates to demonstrate these skills 'live' by interacting with each other.

How many people will take part?

Group exercises are normally designed for between 4–8 candidates.

...and how many assessors?

Throughout the discussion or role play you will be observed by experienced managers from the recruiting company who will decide whether to offer you a job based on your performance (as well as your performance in psychometric tests, interviews and possibly other exercises, such as a presentation). Usually there will be one assessor for every two candidates.

How long will each exercise take?

Group exercises normally last around 50 minutes. Depending on the complexity of the exercise, candidates are normally given a specified period of time before the exercise starts to make themselves familiar with any given background information.

What will assessors be looking for?

Assessors will primarily want to see evidence that you are able to work as part of a team. How successful you are at this will depend on how effectively you can put across your point of view, listen to other people's opinions, challenge others where appropriate, and demonstrate that you have understood the information you were presented with.

What if I'm a shy person? Will I be at a disadvantage?

If you are naturally reserved, the prospect of having to speak up during a group exercise might seem daunting. However, being a talkative person does not always give you an advantage either. It all depends on what you say, and how you treat other people.

There are individuals who dominate every situation and every discussion, never allowing anyone else to get a word in. If there's a person like this in *your* group, don't worry. Hogging the conversation and completely taking over is clearly not a good way to demonstrate either inter-personal sensitivity or the ability to take other people's views on board, so such an individual is unlikely to be successful.

Remember that with group exercises the assessors will be looking for evidence that candidates have taken in the information mentioned in the brief. It's better to come up with a few relevant points than a stream of irrelevant rubbish. On the other hand, if you stay completely silent, the assessors will have little opportunity to evaluate your skills or personality.

Note: to *increase your confidence* you might like to try debating issues with friends, family or work colleagues. If you're at university, perhaps you could join a debating society. If you are currently working, how about exploring the possibility of attending departmental meetings as an observer (or ideally a participant)?

What if I think a task is ridiculous, or irrelevant?

Most private sector assessment centres will not include any physical 'game playing' – the exception here may be for some roles in the Armed Forces or similar. Best practice dictates that all the tests and exercises you participate in as well as the assessment centre experience as a whole, should leave you with control and dignity. Everything that happens should be relevant to the business environment and the job itself.

However, it could happen that you've been asked to do something ridiculous – it's not unheard of for people to be subjected to silly outdoor exercises, crossing imaginary minefields etc., but you don't have to put up with it. You always have a choice.

Either go along with the exercise, always behaving as professionally as possible *or* don't go along with it – remember that the assessment centre is as much about you finding out about the recruiting organisation as being tested by them.

If you're feeling brave, ask what the relevance of the exercise is and then weigh up the reasonableness (or not) of their answer. If it seems to you that the exercise has just been thought up by some overbearing, power mad, game-playing manager out to have a bit of fun at your expense, ask yourself if you really want to work for them at all.

Luckily these days, most companies treat candidates with professionalism and courtesy. You deserve nothing less.

Interviews

These need no introduction, but to cover them in detail would take an entire book! However, if you can answer the following questions confidently you'll do well:

- Why do you want to work for this company?
- Why are you specifically interested in this job?
- What would you contribute to this company?
- What skills would you be bringing to this job?
- In which direction would you like to take the job/the department/the team/this company?
- Why do you want to leave your current job?
- What aspects of your current job do you enjoy the most?
- And the least?
- What are your strengths and weaknesses?
- How well do you work in a team?
- What are your career objectives?
- How long do you plan to stay with our company?
- Where do you see yourself in five years' time?
- Do you have any questions?

You are very unlikely to be able to answer all of these vitally important questions convincingly unless you have a) researched the company (and the industry itself), and b) given thought to the job itself – why you want it, why you'd be good at it and in which direction you want to take it.

Questions about situations in which you have demonstrated particular skills (often referred to as 'competencies') and how you have tackled specific problems are also popular, for example:

- How have you dealt with difficult problems at work? Can you give examples?
- How do you rate yourself as a manager?
- How have you dealt with staff-related performance issues?
- Tell me about an occasion when you made a bad mistake at work? What happened and what did you learn from it?
- How have you ensured your team met an important deadline?

Situational questions (also known as competency questions) are quite popular. Situational questions place you in an imaginary but relevant situation and ask you what your likely action would be. Here's an example:

You are the manager of a team of call centre staff who are all very sociable. After one team night out you come into work and find an 'atmosphere' among the team members. Something obviously happened last night but people in the team are not willing to talk to you about it. What would you do?

Situational questions don't have right or wrong answers; there isn't a perfect response. However what you *do* say will tell an astute interviewer a lot about your managerial style and personality, so answer with care. The trick is to balance respect for other people with the demands of your job while still remaining professional, fair and reasonable.

In this instance, the most likely scenario is that only two people clashed, in which case the whole thing might blow over fairly quickly. How much do you as their manager need to know anyway? It would be presumptuous to interrogate anyone unnecessarily. Pushing for answers could also lead to resentment and show you up as a meddler.

Perhaps you could say that for these very reasons you'd simply wait and see whether anyone's work was affected, and if so, to what extent. Only if it looked like becoming an ongoing issue and *not* an isolated incident would you then try to resolve the problem by having a quiet word with whoever seems the most affected.

To sum up – interviews are an important part of what is (for a managerial position) a very long and rigorous assessment process. At an assessment event you can expect at least one fairly general interview, which could also include a discussion about your test results. Later into the recruitment process at an assessment centre and beyond, you can expect much more intense and lengthier interviews, perhaps with more than one person.

Some of the big city firms have a reputation for putting potential recruits through a succession of multiple interviews. The public sector is known for being particularly keen on the panel interview where (for the most senior positions) you could be interviewed by up to 10 people at the same time!

Management tests and exercises – how to improve your performance

General performance – management skills

◆ If you're already working, take an interest in your current organisation's management. Perhaps you could go along to management meetings and join in with discussions, or talk about management issues with your boss.

◆ If you're still at university or in the middle of a business degree, pick up valuable management experience by joining different clubs, societies or voluntary organisations and playing an active role in them. Don't just go along – offer to help, find out what needs doing and get on with it.

◆ Alternatively, organise your own club or society from scratch. Setting it up, attracting members, organising venues, times and dates, motivating people to get involved and stay involved, dealing with finance – these are all immensely valuable management skills which will not only help you shine whenever you come up against a management test but can be used to greatly enhance your CV as well.

◆ Take an interest in current business news, read the business press and business journals. Apart from the general and financial news, you can often find interesting articles featuring all sorts of prominent business people giving advice on how to tackle specific management problems. Think about how *you* would tackle the problems.

◆ Talk to people you know who work in management or run their own businesses, about the kind of management problems they encounter and how they deal with them. Discuss the issues and ask lots of questions.

◆ Read books on management. Remember that the authors are usually professional writers, not entrepreneurs, and may have little experience of actually running a large company.

◆ During group exercises and role-plays, try not to be distracted or fazed by the assessors and observers. They are just doing their job, not trying to intimidate you. Like you, they'll also be longing for a cup of tea or big stiff drink!

◆ Remember to research the company – see **Chapter Eight** for how to do this.

♦ Research the tools used – e.g. www.shlgroup.com, www.psychtesting.org.uk, www.monster.co.uk.

General performance – social skills

Good social skills are a necessity if you want to become a successful manager. To improve yours, try talking to people you don't know, perhaps at work or social functions. It takes courage for a shy person to introduce themselves or start a conversation with a stranger, but the more you do it, the more relaxed you'll feel. This will give you confidence when it comes to the assessment centre experience and also help you to feel OK about being assertive, or taking the initiative during the group exercises.

Managers are regularly required to interact and discuss a whole range of situations with other managers, customers, suppliers and staff. It's never too late to start working on those communication skills.

Finally, always treat the assessors and other candidates with courtesy and respect. Who knows, you could be working alongside them in the future.

PART THREE
Personality Questionnaires

CHAPTER ELEVEN

Personality Questionnaires

What are personality questionnaires?

Personality questionnaires are psychometric tests which assess the different aspects of personality and character which are relevant to the world of work, for example:

- ✓ motivation
- ✓ thinking style
- ✓ problem-solving
- ✓ preferred working style
- ✓ feelings and emotions
- ✓ business awareness
- ✓ interpersonal skills
- ✓ leadership ability
- ✓ managerial, professional or entrepreneurial qualities
- ✓ communication skills.

However, personality questionnaires, or 'inventories' or 'self report forms' as they are sometimes called, are not tests in the true sense of the word, for two reasons:

1 there are no right or wrong answers
2 they are not timed.

They are, however, popular. Written by occupational psychologists and administered by trained HR personnel, their use has increased dramatically in the last few years. From shelf-stacker to managing director, apply for a job with any medium to large organisation (commercial or otherwise) and I can virtually guarantee you will be asked to complete one or more personality questionnaire.

The results of the personality questionnaire could determine your overall suitability to work for a particular organisation, or place you in an appropriate department, or team once the decision has already been made to employ you. They're also very useful for recruiters, because it gives them something to talk about when they interview you.

Used in conjunction with ability-type tests, personality questionnaires can give an employer a pretty accurate assessment of how well you would be suited to a particular job.

There are **two** main types of personality questionnaire. The first is often referred to in HR jargon as a 'competency' questionnaire.

Competency questionnaires

Competency questionnaires tend to be pretty short, and they focus on behavioural actions, which are things like:

◆ Managerial qualities (leadership, planning, organisation, attention to detail and persuasiveness).
◆ Professional qualities (specialist knowledge, problem-solving, analytical ability, oral and written communication).
◆ Entrepreneurial qualities (commercial awareness, creativity, understanding of the need to plan for the longer term).
◆ Personal qualities (an ability to work well with other people, flexibility, resilience and motivation).

Competency questionnaires are frequently used on application forms and online application forms. Here's an example of the sort of question you might get:

I am the sort of person who....

1 A Easily establishes rapport with reports.
   B Influences the course of meetings.
   C Speaks coherently.
   D Encourages colleagues to meet objectives.

2　A　Writes creatively.

　　B　Seeks answers to problems.

　　C　Is effective in communicating requirements.

　　D　Is aware of costs.

For each question you have to decide which statement is the most like you and also which is the least like you – not an easy task.

Competency-type questions are also a favourite with interviewers who, analysing the answers you gave on the application form test, like to hit you with questions like:

'*Tell me about a situation in which you influenced the course of a meeting.*'

You can see what they're getting at; they want to know how you behave in the work situation.

The way competency questionnaires are scored is that generally, each organisation using them chooses a small number of qualities which they feel are essential to the particular job, and use these to put together their own unique scoring key. This is very sensible, since nobody in the world has all the qualities listed above.

So if you are rejected by a company on the basis of an application form test, don't worry. You might be the 'wrong' sort of person for them, but perfect for the next company you apply to. I'd say it's best to forget about the scoring mechanism and just answer as honestly as you can, because it's in your interest to do so.

True personality questionnaires

True personality questionnaires are usually much longer than competency-type questionnaires. For example, one version of SHL's very well known *OPQ* 32, which asks you to answer questions in a similar format to the Making Choices test shown below, has 108 pages!

Personality questionnaires are generally used when you go along to be interviewed, when you attend an assessment centre, and they are often completed online. The SHL tests are scored by measuring the test result against 32 different dimensions of personality. These include:

- Relationships with people (how persuasive, controlling, outgoing, modest, caring, democratic, independently minded, confident or outspoken you are).

- Your thinking style (how rational, evaluative, conventional, conceptual, innovative, forward thinking, detail conscious, conscientious or rule following you are).

- Your feelings and emotions (how relaxed, worrying, tough minded, optimistic, trusting, emotionally controlled, vigorous, competitive, achieving or decisive you are).

All of these 'dimensions' are related to how you behave in the workplace.

How can personality questionnaires be valid when candidates rate themselves?

Recruiting organisations are fully aware that personality questionnaires reveal only your *perception* of yourself, which isn't necessarily the same thing as the way other people see you. However, the tests are very sophisticated, and in most cases (as I have found out recently myself) frighteningly accurate.

Will I be asked any very personal questions?

No, you shouldn't be. Personality questionnaires are not puzzles or quizzes of the magazine variety; they never ask you about your favourite foods or your love life. The personality questionnaires used in recruitment simply assess aspects of your personality and character as they relate to the working environment, or a specific job.

What sort of questions will I be asked?

To give you a flavour of what to expect I have included two different practice personality questionnaires for you to try. As mentioned above, the only difference between these tests and the real thing is that real-live personality questionnaires have a lot more questions. Try to answer the questions honestly and accurately – it's not easy, as you will see.

Test 34 Rating Statements

In this test you are asked to rate yourself on a number of different phrases or statements. After reading each statement mark your answer according to the following rules:

Fill in circle 1   If you strongly disagree with the statement
Fill in circle 2   If you disagree with the statement
Fill in circle 3   If you are unsure
Fill in circle 4   If you agree with the statement
Fill in circle 5   If you strongly agree with the statement

The first statement has already been completed for you. The person has agreed that 'I enjoy meeting new people' is an accurate description of him/herself.

Now try questions 2 to 6 for yourself by completely filling in the circle that is most true for you.

		Strongly disagree	Disagree	Unsure	Agree	Strongly agree
1	I enjoy meeting new people	①	②	③	●	⑤
2	I like helping people	①	②	③	④	⑤
3	I sometimes make mistakes	①	②	③	④	⑤
4	I don't mind taking risks	①	②	③	④	⑤
5	I'm easily disappointed	①	②	③	④	⑤
6	I enjoy repairing things	①	②	③	④	⑤

Test 35 Making choices

This personality questionnaire is similar to the well known SHL *OPQ* 32. For each question you are given a block of four statements: A, B, C and D. You must choose the statement which you think is *most* true or typical of you in your everyday behaviour, and you must **also** choose the statement which is *least* true or typical of you.

Indicate your choices by filling in the appropriate circle in the row marked 'M' (for most) and in the next row 'L' (for least).

The first question has been completed as an example of what to do. The person has chosen, '*I feel relaxed*' as most true or typical, and '*I am organised*' as being least true or typical. Now try the rest yourself, thinking carefully before you answer.

1   A   I am outgoing

    B   I feel relaxed

    C   I am determined to win

    C   I am organised

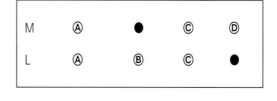

2   A   I like helping people

    B   I enjoy competitive activities

    C   I view things positively

    D   I like to follow procedures

3   A   I criticise openly

    B   I put great emphasis on other's views

    C   I need people's company

    D   I follow established work methods

4   A   I enjoy organising events

    B   I sometimes get angry

    C   I am talkative

    D   I resolve conflicts at work

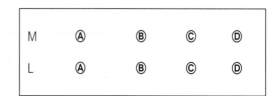

5 A I am seldom quiet

   B I focus on underlying concepts   M   Ⓐ   Ⓑ   Ⓒ   Ⓓ

   C I am free of tension   L   Ⓐ   Ⓑ   Ⓒ   Ⓓ

   D I sell a new idea well

6 A I enjoy variety

   B I am highly active   M   Ⓐ   Ⓑ   Ⓒ   Ⓓ

   C I get the details right   L   Ⓐ   Ⓑ   Ⓒ   Ⓓ

   D I am effective in negotiations

7 A I quickly consider the options

   B I am bored by routine   M   Ⓐ   Ⓑ   Ⓒ   Ⓓ

   C I like to understand the underlying theory   L   Ⓐ   Ⓑ   Ⓒ   Ⓓ

   D I am ambitious

8 A I keep paperwork in order

   B I need to win   M   Ⓐ   Ⓑ   Ⓒ   Ⓓ

   C I insist on doing this my own way   L   Ⓐ   Ⓑ   Ⓒ   Ⓓ

   D I get worried before a big meeting

9 A I have a wide circle of friends

   B I enjoy organising people   M   Ⓐ   Ⓑ   Ⓒ   Ⓓ

   C I relax easily   L   Ⓐ   Ⓑ   Ⓒ   Ⓓ

   D I seek variety

10 A   I raise hypothetical arguments

   B   I follow my own approach despite others' views

   C   I find negotiation easy

   D   I am tense before an interview

	A	B	C	D
M	Ⓐ	Ⓑ	Ⓒ	Ⓓ
L	Ⓐ	Ⓑ	Ⓒ	Ⓓ

11 A   I like statistical analysis

   B   I take a conventional approach

   C   I draw immediate conclusions

   D   I rarely lose or misplace things

	A	B	C	D
M	Ⓐ	Ⓑ	Ⓒ	Ⓓ
L	Ⓐ	Ⓑ	Ⓒ	Ⓓ

12 A   I set long-term objectives

   B   I take a methodical approach

   C   I conceal my emotions

   D   I critically evaluate a piece of work

	A	B	C	D
M	Ⓐ	Ⓑ	Ⓒ	Ⓓ
L	Ⓐ	Ⓑ	Ⓒ	Ⓓ

13 A   I enjoy bargaining with someone

   B   I take time to be supportive

   C   I speak up when people are wrong

   D   I quickly draw conclusions

	A	B	C	D
M	Ⓐ	Ⓑ	Ⓒ	Ⓓ
L	Ⓐ	Ⓑ	Ⓒ	Ⓓ

14 A   I keep things tidy

   B   I produce innovative solutions

   C   I like to work with numbers

   D   I make it clear when I disagree

	A	B	C	D
M	Ⓐ	Ⓑ	Ⓒ	Ⓓ
L	Ⓐ	Ⓑ	Ⓒ	Ⓓ

What if I can't decide which statement is *least* like me?

I agree, it is difficult. In the past, when you took a personality test, there would always be several answer choices which stood out a mile as being the wrong ones. But not any more.

Here are some other examples of statements taken from personality questionnaires:

◆ Changes tasks willingly and grasps new ideas quickly.
◆ Communicates equally well with customers and colleagues.
◆ Pursues tasks energetically.
◆ Shares all relevant and useful information with the team.

You can see the problem. Which of these statements should you choose as being the *least* like you? They all describe qualities you'd imagine any employer would find highly desirable.

This test, and others like it are extremely clever because they are impossible to fudge. There are no obvious right or wrong answers. And the fact that there are no blindingly obvious 'least like you' answers, forces you to think hard about yourself and be honest.

And that's exactly what organisations who use these tests want – honesty.

Note: you may have problems deciding which statements are *most* like you too!

Is it possible to cheat?

Modern personality questionnaires have sophisticated built-in mechanisms which can spot any deliberate lying or inconsistency easily. If you try to second guess the examiners by picking the answers you think they're looking for, your questionnaire is likely to be regarded as invalid and your application rejected. Your only choice is to answer the questions as truthfully and honestly as you can.

The tests also have a huge number of questions and the sheer size of the questionnaire makes it even more difficult to lie consistently – it might be possible at the beginning, but by the 100th question it'll be difficult to remember your own name, let alone which qualities you're pretending to possess!

Besides, personality questionnaires are also about fitting the right people into the right jobs. By answering honestly, you're more likely to land a job that you enjoy and can do well.

Are there any other types of personality questionnaire?

In this chapter I have covered competency and personality questionnaires, however you could also be asked to complete an **interest inventory**, which is a questionnaire in which you are asked to decide how much you like various types of activities at work.

You could also come across something called a **motivation questionnaire** which looks at the energy with which you approach your work, and the different conditions which increase or decrease your motivation. Personally I think that as far as motivation is concerned, your employer has a lot to answer for!

Personality questionnaires – how to improve your performance

With every other type of psychometric test I have been able to give you some suggestions as to how to improve your performance, however with personality questionnaires, there are no tricks of the trade or useful exercises to practise. As I have already said, the most important thing to do is to *be yourself*. Remember:

◆ Personality and competency questionnaires do not have right or wrong answers. You don't have to worry about passing or failing – just concentrate on being honest, truthful and accurate.

◆ Make sure you answer all the questions. There may seem like a lot of them, but it *is* necessary to complete the whole test.

◆ Personality questionnaires do not have time limits, but try to work your way through reasonably quickly. This is particularly useful when being asked to decide which 'qualities' are most or least like you as intuitive answers are usually the most accurate.

◆ Some questions may seem irrelevant. Don't worry about this. Just answer as truthfully as you can and move on. The same goes for questions you don't fully understand. Do your best and don't leave any of the answers blank.

◆ Many questions ask you about the way you behave in a work situation. If you have no formal work experience, think about how you behave in similar situation at university or college or other areas of your life.

◆ As mentioned above, many big firms actually list the personality traits they look for in their employees on their websites. Treat this information as a useful guide but don't try to second-guess the examiner – always be honest.

◆ After you've finished the test, you might have second thoughts about some of your responses. For example, after taking the *OPQ* 32 I suddenly realised that rating all the 'I plan ahead' type statements as *least* like me was totally inaccurate; I should have chosen *most* like me instead! Everyone does this, but be assured it doesn't seem to affect the test results greatly.

After taking a personality questionnaire, you should be offered the chance to discuss the results (and if the offer is not forthcoming, ask). Use the opportunity to find out as much about yourself as you can. Even if you are not offered that particular position, a better understanding of your strengths and limitations is always useful.

CHAPTER TWELVE

What Else Does All This Testing Measure?

As you have seen, there are many different types of tests you will encounter during your journey into management. Some measure your ability to work or reason in a certain way, some claim to analyse aspects of your personality and character, others test your ability to manage people, evaluate and solve problems, or make sound business decisions.

But there are three things that all these recruitment tests measure:

♦ Firstly, your ability to concentrate and work hard for a reasonable amount of time, even when under considerable pressure.

♦ Secondly, your ability to follow instructions to the letter.

♦ And lastly, your ability (or lack of it) to understand precisely what you are being asked to do.

These are qualities **every** organisation looks for in its senior staff. Managing isn't just about making important business decisions. The role of management could also be said to include upholding an organisation's ethos and culture, following existing laid-down procedures and not making up your own rules as you go along, acting professionally and responsibly at all times, setting a good example to more junior staff...the list is endless.

All these tests give employers confidence that they've chosen the right people. Not only that, it gives them confidence that they've gone about it in a reasonably fair and objective way, which they have, because...

As everyone knows, your references may not be entirely honest. Your CV may exaggerate your achievements or completely omit items you're not so proud of. A sparkling performance at interview has been known to pull the wool over many an interviewer's eyes. But with psychometric, personality and management testing, you are on your own. You can see why employers like them so much.

PART FOUR
Avoiding the Assessment Process Altogether

CHAPTER THIRTEEN

Avoiding Psychometric and Management Tests Altogether

What if, despite hours of practice, the thought of taking a psychometric test or participating in yet another 'group exercise' or 'businesses simulation' makes you feel like running for the hills? Is it possible to avoid having to take psychometric and management tests altogether?

Well, given that a growing number of companies subject potential employees to some sort of testing in addition to the traditional face-to-face interview, it may not be possible to do this, especially if you are applying for a management position in a large company.

However, there are a number of possibilities that do spring to mind. The most obvious one is to apply for a job with an SME.

Working for an SME

Before you decide that the only organisations worth working for are big ones, consider the alternative. A smaller company (an SME) may have just as much, or even more to offer.

Note: The definition of an SME varies according to who you ask! To give you a rough guide, an SME is usually an organisation which employs up to 50 people, and/or a turnover up to £20 million. So 'small' can mean anything from absolutely tiny, to really quite large, well-established and vastly successful companies.

Here are just some of the advantages of working for an SME:

✓ More responsibility, earlier on.
✓ The chance to work directly with the directors or owners of the business.
✓ Greater variety of work.
✓ The opportunity to learn every aspect of how a business works.
✓ Reasonable salaries (SMEs know they have to compete with the big boys).

✓   A real chance to be a big fish in a small pond.

It's also much easier to land a job with an SME than a large company because their recruitment processes are usually simpler. After you've submitted your CV and letter, huge numbers of SMEs still rely on a couple of interviews to pick their people, even top management. Of course, I can't absolutely guarantee that. An ability test to determine your suitability for a specific is still a very real possibility. But with an SME you are certainly less likely to be given a psychometric test, and very unlikely to be required to attend an assessment centre, give a presentation, or have your Lego building capabilities scrutinised.

Just why this should be so isn't clear. Perhaps it's because most SMEs (and certainly the smaller ones) do not possess full-time personnel departments, or the time and resources to drag the recruitment process out for longer than absolutely necessary. Perhaps it's the considerable cost of putting potential recruits through a full-blown assessment centre process that puts them off.

Perhaps it's because directors of small firms, who often interview applicants themselves, are confident about their abilities to pick the right people without recourse to additional methods of selection. I call it the '*I can recognise the right candidate as soon as he/she walks in,*' syndrome. Whether it works or not, thousands of company directors still suffer from it; a situation psychometric and management test publishers are working very hard to change.

So before they succeed, I would definitely recommend you consider working for an SME.

Working for yourself

What if management appeals, but not the ideas of anyone else making decisions which affect you? What if you'd welcome responsibility, but 'team player' isn't in your vocabulary?

Funnily enough, many of the world's most successful entrepreneurs would not only fail miserably at an assessment centre, they'd probably be considered completely unemployable.

If you've just recognised yourself, then perhaps becoming self-employed could be for you. It would certainly appeal if you are the sort of person who:

- likes the autonomy of making his or her own decisions.
- is happy to work alone, at least some of the time.
- is extremely determined.
- is prepared to forgo the security of a guaranteed salary, at least in the early stages.

Successful entrepreneurs also have to be very organised and hard working. They are frequently charismatic and creative risk-takers with leadership ability. They are usually confident (but not necessarily extravert), always intelligent, with the ability to get on well with others when occasion demands.

And because fashions, industries and economies are constantly changing, successful entrepreneurs also have to be prepared to face a never-ending stream of challenges and problems. However, if you have a product or service that people want, and you are able to offer a professional and reliable service, there's every chance that in time, you could become very successful indeed.

And if you did, well you'd really be 'managing' in the real sense of the word. You would make the decisions. You would hold the purse strings. And you would take the risks – a completely different situation from working as a line manager inside a huge organisation, however fancy your title is.

Of course, working for yourself has its downside too. You will have to market your product or service in order to find customers which can be very difficult. You may not have a boss telling you what to do, but you'll still have masters: fickle customers, unreliable suppliers, and whoever you've borrowed money from looking over your shoulder. Furthermore, it may take a long time to build up a regular clientele, which means your income stays lower for longer than your employed friends.

But one thing is certain: if you work for yourself, no one will ever expect you to take a psychometric test!

For help and advice on becoming self-employed, try:

- Business Link www.businesslink.gov.uk
- Inland Revenue www.inlandrevenue.gov.uk/startingup
- Small Business Service www.sbs.gov.uk
- The DTI www.dti.gov.uk
- Federation of Small Businesses www.fsb.org.uk
- www.bizhelp24.com
- The Prince's Trust Business Club www.princes-trust.org

- www.bt.com/getstarted
- Your relevant trade organisation.
- **Plus**: talk to people you know who are already running their own businesses. Ask them about their experiences and the problems they've faced. They'll soon bring you down to earth if your expectations are unrealistic.

Resources

Help and information on the Internet

www.shldirect.com

Easy to navigate site includes careers guidance, help with the assessment process and free practice ability tests and personality questionnaires.

www.psychtesting.org.uk

Informative site on psychometric testing includes practice tests.

www.psychometrics.co.uk

Interesting information about psychometric tests, assessment centres, CV writing etc.

www.advisorteam.com

Take the free Keirsey Temperament Sorter and discover whether you are an Artisan, Guardian, Rational or Idealist. Also IQ tests.

www.testingroom.com

US site offering free tests on topics such as personality, career values, career interest inventories and career competencies.

www.majon.com/iq.html

Another interesting US site includes IQ test selection area and high-level psychometric tests.

www.9types.com

Entertaining personality questionnaire site.

http://www.outofservice.com/

All sorts of personality tests, not particularly work-based but good fun nevertheless.

Job sites

There are thousands of job sites listing management positions, these are just a few of my favourites:

www.monster.co.uk

Massive job site with career advice.

www.prospects.ac.uk

Fantastic graduate career website has help and information for everyone, not just grads.

www.topjobs.co.uk

UK-based job site has lots of management-level jobs.

www.hotrecruit.co.uk

Forget the management job and get something extraordinary or crazy instead!

www.jobserve.com

Good recruitment site for a multitude of different industries, especially IT.

Business information

www.bizhelp24.com

An amazing UK business and finance resource covering every business issue including credit, cash flow, loans, bankruptcy, home working etc.

www.businesslink.gov.uk

Practical help and advice on all aspects of UK business.

To find any company website, either use an intelligent search engine such as www.google.co.uk, or try www.kellysearch.com

UK newspapers with searchable news and business online archives:

www.guardian.co.uk
www.independent.co.uk
www.ft.com
www.thetimes.co.uk

www.companieshouse.gov.uk
Download latest filed accounts and other financial information on approximately two million UK companies.

More company information available from:
www.keynote.co.uk
www.mintel.co.uk

Start-up information

Inland Revenue www.inlandrevenue.gov.uk/startingup
Small Business Service www.sbs.gov.uk
The DTI www.dti.gov.uk
Federation of Small Businesses www.fsb.org.uk
www.bizhelp24.com
The Prince's Trust Business Club www.princes-trust.org
www.bt.com/getstarted

Further reading

Be Prepared!, Julie-Ann Amos (How To Books). Getting ready for job interviews.

Career Change Handbook, The, Graham Green (How To Books). How to find out what you're good at and enjoy and get someone to pay you for it.

CVs for High Flyers, Rachel Bishop-Firth (How To Books). Elevate your career with a CV that gets you noticed.

Graduate Career Directory (Hobsons). Career and job hunting advice plus hundreds of employer profiles.

Handling Tough Job Interviews, Julie-Ann Amos (How To Books). Be prepared, perform well, get the job.

High Powered CVs, Rachel Bishop-Firth (How To Books). Powerful application strategies to get you that senior level job.

Landing Your First Job, Andrea Shavick (Kogan Page). Step-by-step guide through the job-hunting maze from CV to interview technique.

Pass that Interview, Judith Johnstone (How To Books). Your systematic guide to coming out on top.

Passing Psychometric Tests, Andrea Shavick (How To Books). How to pass the tests, whether you're a school leaver, graduate, already working or a returner.

Practice Psychometric Tests Andrea Shavick (How To Books). Lots of practice at every level.

Psychometric Tests for Graduates, Andrea Shavick (How To Books). Graduate-level psychometric and management tests.

Succeeding at Interviews, Judith Verity (How To Books). Give great answers and ask the right questions.

Successful Interviews Every Time, Rob Yeung (How To Books). Be confident of making a great impression and acing that job interview.

Ultimate CV for Managers and Professionals, The, Rachel Bishop-Firth (How To Books). Win senior managerial positions with an outstanding resumé.

Write a Great CV, Paul McGee (How To Books). Prepare a powerful CV that really works.

Write a Winning CV, Julie-Ann Amos (How To Books). Essential CV writing skills that will get you the job you want.

A Guide to taking Psychometric Tests for Visually Impaired Individuals, <u>Royal National Institute for the Blind (RNIB)</u>

Index